Culinary Expeditions

A CELEBRATION OF FOOD AND CULTURE
Inspired by Penn Museum Treasures

Produced by **The Women's Committee**
to benefit the **University of Pennsylvania Museum of Archaeology and Anthropology**

Published and Distributed by
The Women's Committee, University of Pennsylvania Museum of Archaeology and Anthropology
3260 South Street, Philadelphia, PA 19104
215.898.9202 | www.penn.museum

Book design ©Suzanne J. McDevitt

Published and printed in the United States of America.

ISBN: 978-0-615-89493-5

From the Director

Julian Siggers, Ph.D.
Williams Director
**University of Pennsylvania Museum
of Archaeology and Anthropology**

As Director of the University of Pennsylvania Museum of Archaeology and Anthropology, it is with great pleasure that I introduce to you the Women's Committee's book, *Culinary Expeditions: A Celebration of Food and Culture Inspired by Penn Museum Treasures.* More than just a collection of recipes, this beautifully illustrated volume integrates culture with cuisine and incorporates photographs of objects housed in the Museum.

The Penn Museum is known for its diversity of archaeological and anthropological material and *Culinary Expeditions* reflects this through its collection of recipes that span both time and space. Curiosity—intellectual and otherwise—is deeply ingrained in the Museum's character, and this book is sure to whet the appetite.

The Women's Committee has promoted the Museum's mission since 1937, and we are grateful to have their support in bringing a love of archaeology and anthropology to audiences throughout Philadelphia and beyond. I offer my sincerest congratulations to the group for their work in creating this book, as it fosters the exact kind of curiosity that the Museum thrives on. It is through this important endeavor that the Women's Committee has extended this curiosity beyond our Museum walls.

Best wishes,

Julian Siggers, Ph.D.
Williams Director

About the Penn Museum

The story of humankind is at the heart of a visit to the Penn Museum, where you can take a remarkable journey through time and across continents. Founded in 1887 and based in Philadelphia, the internationally renowned University of Pennsylvania Museum of Archaeology and Anthropology has conducted more than 300 research expeditions around the world, and has collected roughly one million objects. Three gallery floors feature materials from ancient Egypt, the Near East, Mesopotamia, Central America, Asia, and the ancient Mediterranean World, as well as artifacts from Native peoples of North America and Africa. The Museum also features a rich calendar of special events and activities for adults, families, and children. Located on the University of Pennsylvania campus across from Franklin Field, the Penn Museum's grand, Italianate-style building has many eclectic features, including Tiffany mosaics, vaulted ceilings, and a massive rotunda. Garden entrances with fountains and a koi pond provide tranquil green spaces for relaxation. Embark on your own culinary expedition with a visit to the Penn Museum and see the artifacts pictured here first-hand.

For more information visit the Museum's website at www.penn.museum or call 215.898.4000.

About the Women's Committee

In 1937 a small group of women formed the Women's Committee to stimulate interest in the Penn Museum's research and educational programs.

Today, visitors to the Museum still benefit from the efforts of these capable, energetic, far-sighted women who began the tradition of initiating, developing, and supporting new projects wherever they saw a need. This tradition continues with the publication of *Culinary Expeditions,* a book that celebrates eight cultural areas represented in the Museum.

Women's Committee initiatives have included the hands-on sorting of artifacts; helping curators in storage; furnishing a Conservation Laboratory; underwriting training of a Conservator; organizing tours to archaeological sites all over the world; establishing a Volunteer Guides program, which later took Museum artifacts directly to schools; opening a Café and a Shop; publishing for 30 years the Members' Newsletter; improving the appearance of the Museum by providing flower arrangements at entrances; and organizing countless lunches, dinners, auctions, and galas.

From 2005 through 2008, the Committee concentrated its efforts on *Treasures,* a multi-cultural antique show and, in 2012, on a four-day *Treasures Jewelry Sale and Show*—all to raise awareness and funds while bringing old and new friends to the Museum. All of the proceeds from the sale of *Culinary Expeditions* will benefit the Penn Museum.

Committee Chair
Nancy Freeman Tabas

Book Committee Chair
Cheryl Louise Baker

Committee
Joan Bachman
Jo Anne S. Bagnell
Peggy Ballinger
Mona Batt
Ann M. Beal
Anne Butcher
Beth Butler
Susan W. Catherwood
Joan I. Coale
Joanne H. Conrad
Bonnie Derr
Maude de Schauensee
Janet Dougherty
Perry Durkin
Beth Fluke
Betty S. Gerstley
Anna Gniotek
Marguerite Goff

Ellen Goldstine
Criswell Gonzalez
Ingrid Graham
Ann Greene
Mary Bert Gutman
Kate Hall
Nancy Hastings
Suchinda Heavener
Joan Holmes
Josephine Hueber
Patricia Hueber
Anne V. Iskrant
Esther Johnson
Pamela C. Keon
Nancy Kneeland
DruEllen Kolker
Virginia Kricun
Doranne M. Lackman
Joyce Lewis

Alida Lovell
Mary Ann Marks
Missy McQuiston
Rosa Meyers
Margy Meyerson
Jack T. Murray
Arlene Olson
Gretchen Riley
Barbara Rittenhouse
Lisa K. Siegel
Trudy Slade
Ann Spaeth
Dodie Trescher
Helen S. Weary
Nancy Bendiner Weiss
Ellen Winn
Helen Winston
Schuy Wood

Book Committee

Book Concept and Design
Suzanne J. McDevitt

Editorial Staff
Jane Hickman
Joan I. Coale
Katherine Boas
Mark Curchack
Deborah S. Dempsey
Amanda Ball

Recipes
Cheryl Louise Baker
Ardeth P. Anderson

Marketing
Lisa K. Siegel
Trudy Slade
Schuy Wood

Recipe Contributors and Testers
Lauren Abshire
Ardeth P. Anderson
Drs. Benjamin and Jane Ashcom
Cheryl Louise Baker
Jackie and Reed Baker
Kaya Ottaviano Bellasis
Robert Berner
Anna Y. Boas
Todd Carson
Susan W. Catherwood
Joan I. Coale
Adrian Copeland
Cynthia Crist-John
Ellen and Rich Cutshall
Ellen S. and Bob DeMarinis
Bonnie Derr
Prema Deshmukh
Erica Fae
Mary Beth Flannigan
Molly Gleeson
Maureen Deeney Goldsmith
Nancy Gordon
Lisa Reifsnyder Gruber
Angie Hafner
Becca Haggerty
Suchinda Heavener
Jane Hickman
Amina Hovey
Ellen J. Hovey-Copeland
DruEllen Kolker
Becky Levy
Therese Marmion
Missy McQuiston
Francis T. Miller
Naomi Miller
Ginny Minehart
Kate Kern Mundie
Nancy Naftulin
Nina Owczarek
Nicholas Parrotta
Jennifer Reifsteck
Jane Reznik
Hannah Rich
Barbara Rittenhouse
Charlotte Rose
Ilene S. Rosen
Mark Rosen
Anna B. Rubin
Toby Schwait
Jonathan Scott
Lisa K. Siegel
Julian Siggers
Rebecca Silver
Trudy Slade
Ann Spaeth
Elizabeth Tabas
Nancy Freeman Tabas
 and Lee Tabas
Phyllis Tallos-Goldring
John Ventura
Martha Witte
Schuy Wood

Financial Support

Jo Anne S. Bagnell
Cheryl Louise Baker
Ann M. Beal
Anne Butcher
Beth Butler
Susan W. Catherwood
Joan I. Coale
Janet Dougherty
Betty S. Gerstley
Mary Bert Gutman
Nancy Hastings
Suchinda Heavener
Joan Holmes
Josephine Hueber
DruEllen Kolker
Barbara Krancer
Hope Makler
Missy McQuiston
Rosa Meyers
Barbara Rittenhouse
Trudy Slade
Ann Spaeth
Nancy Freeman Tabas
Helen S. Weary
Helen Winston
Schuy Wood

Special Acknowledgments

Katherine Blanchard
Ann Brownlee
Jennifer Chiappardi
Elin Danien
Maureen Deeney Goldsmith
Pam Kosty
Stephen Lang
Dwaune Latimer
Lynn Makowsky
Simon Martin
James Mathieu
Patrick McGovern
Naomi Miller
Amanda Mitchell-Boyask
Janet Monge
Katherine Moore
Alessandro Pezzati
Jennifer Quick
C. Brian Rose
Francine Sarin
Eric Schnittke
David P. Silverman
Adam Smith
Melissa Smith
Thomas Stanley
Loa Traxler
Jennifer Houser Wegner
William Wierzbowski
Lucy Fowler Williams
Richard Zettler

Contents

Contents

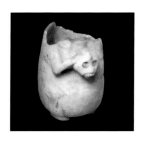

Contents

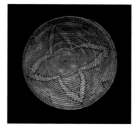

What is BCE/CE?
You will see the abbreviations BCE and CE associated with dates in this book. BCE (Before Common Era) is used to replace BC (Before Christ), and CE (Common Era) replaces AD (Anno Domini—"In the year of our Lord").

This system provides a religiously neutral way to reference dates within the Gregorian calendar.

*The mere smell of cooking
can evoke a whole civilization.*

— Fernand Braudel

Introduction

A culture's cuisine is as intimately tied to its identity as are geographic or political boundaries. But the difference between food and geopolitics is this: whereas boundaries are drawn to create exclusivity, food brings people together. Meals are the anchors of social interaction. *Culinary Expeditions* aims to be both informative and instructional on this point, examining world cultures through their culinary traditions, and is aligned with the mission of the University of Pennsylvania Museum of Archaeology and Anthropology to promote an understanding of the world's cultural heritage. Above all, it is the hope of the Women's Committee of the Penn Museum that the recipes contained in this book will inspire readers to broaden their culinary and cultural horizons.

A good book, like a good dish, requires the right ingredients. In *Culinary Expeditions* you will find authentic recipes that are accessible for the modern cook. We feature recipes from eight regions of the world, all represented in the collection at the Penn Museum. In a sense, the creation of this book was an expedition unto itself. We made considerable efforts to research the cultural origins of each region's cuisine, making use of Museum resources and seeking the guidance of experts when necessary. The result is something beyond the typical cookbook. Each section's introductory cultural material provides insight into each region's attitude towards food and, by extension, their outlook on life. When you read *Culinary Expeditions*, you will gain more than the promise of many tasty future meals. You will gain a new appreciation for the food that sustains culture.

—The Editors

Artifact

OSTRICH EGG SHELL CONTAINER

Botswana

Early 20th century CE

Africa

Within its vast size—three times the continental U.S.—Africa includes a startling variety of peoples and practices. Foodways range from the simplest of roasting or boiling of gathered roots and fruits to highly elaborate cuisines rich in spices and a variety of ingredients. While there are numerous indigenous crops with great nutritional value, many foods consumed today are grains and tubers introduced by colonizers, missionaries, and traders from Europe, Asia, the Pacific, and the Americas.

Africa is still the most rural continent. Most Africans are farmers, raising crops for their own consumption, and, if there is a surplus, for sale in the market. Small domestic animals such as goats and chickens provide meat and eggs, and villagers supplement their diets by hunting, fishing, and gathering what products can be found nearby. In the savannah regions, which constitute about 30% of the continent, the predominant crops are grains—millet, sorghum (native grasses), maize, rice (from the Americas and Asia, respectively)—and pulses such as peanuts and beans, and melons. In the more forested regions (i.e. 20% of the land) we also find corn and rice, plus cassava, bananas, and yams, all introduced crops. Grains are often made into porridges or ground into flour, which is then made into dough or fried into cakes. *Ugali,* a cornmeal mush, is a common dish. Likewise, peanuts and other beans make their way into soups and stews or are ground for other uses. The roots and fruits of the forest are also turned into soups. Fish, eaten fried or in stews, is consumed by peoples living near rivers or coastal areas. Quite often foods are very liberally spiced with chili peppers, a New World import.

A significant alternative to the farming lifestyle is found among the pastoralist peoples who herd their cattle throughout the great swath of grassland that runs in a giant arc from below the Sahara and down the East African Rift Valley to the veldts of South Africa. These are the Fulani of West Africa; the Somali and Nuer of the Horn of Africa

Artifact

PEANUT-SHAPED GOLD WEIGHT

Ghana, Africa
20th century CE

Ostrich Egg Shell Container
Associated with the Bushmen culture, this large ostrich egg shell includes scratched decoration. After the contents were eaten (the equivalent of 18-24 chicken eggs), it was used as a water container. Museum object #31-2-134

Peanut-Shaped Gold Weight
This Ashanti "gold weight" is actually made of brass. Manufactured in the shape of a peanut, it was used as a counterweight in the weighing of gold dust. Museum object #AF2399A

and Sudan; the Maasai, Samburu, Turkana, and Karimojong of Kenya and Tanzania; the Khoi-Khoi of Botswana; and others. Cattle, probably introduced down the Nile Valley, are the source of wealth for these people and thus are eaten only when they die naturally. The Maasai people consume the milk and blood of their cattle, renewable resources. Some groups practice limited agriculture, but the need to find grazing generally keeps communities on the move.

Cuisines vary considerably by region and by the type of foods available in this enormous continent. In North Africa—Egypt and west across the Mediterranean littoral—preparations have much in common with the Middle East, reflecting the spread of Arab culture to these areas: for example, meats and vegetables grilled on skewers, beans ground or in pastes, roasted vegetables with flat bread, sweet cakes of honey, and phyllo pastry. In Morocco this style is elaborated and is characterized by meat, fish, or vegetable stews, often with fruits and sweet spices, cooked in a special conical ceramic pot called a *tagine*. The immense expanse of the Sahara is populated by camel nomads, the Tuaregs, who have navigated these spaces for centuries. A Tuareg feast features a sheep roasted so slowly that the meat flakes off in one's hand.

In the sub-Saharan savannah zone known as the Sahel, the common foods are the porridges and boiled or baked cakes mentioned above, seasoned with small amounts of meat if available. The exceptions occur on festival days when domestic animals may be slaughtered and roasted; this expenditure of resources is part of what makes those days special. The forest zone along the Gulf of Guinea has a more varied diet, with fish (fried or stewed) and fruits along with the cereal products. Where starchy crops are grown, principally cassava and yam, the staple of the cuisine is *fufu*—a gooey paste made of the ground-up tuber and water, formed into bite-sized balls and dipped into soups or sauces. This technique is widespread, reaching from West Africa through Central Africa. In the Lake District (Rwanda, Burundi, and Uganda) and in southern Africa, the nearly identical product is known as *ugali*.

The highlands of Ethiopia are home to a distinctive cuisine which has become better known in the West. It centers around pancakes made with the fermented batter of the local grain called *tef*. The *injira*, as these pancakes are called, which are akin to a flattened *fufu*, serves both as the base atop which the various meat and vegetable stews

---

Benin Rooster Statue
This bronze sculpture, 52 centimeters or over 20 inches tall, is from the Edo culture of the Benin Kingdom. It was created using the lost-wax casting method and contains many carefully rendered surface details. Museum object #AF2065A

Artifact

BENIN ROOSTER STATUE

Nigeria

18th century CE

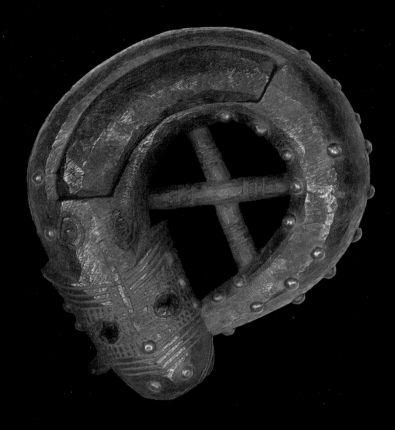

Artifact

EDO KOLA NUT BOX

Nigeria

19th century CE

are placed and as an implement to scoop them up. Traditionally, the stews are spiced well beyond the capacities of most Western diners. Ethiopia is most likely the home of coffee, and the Ethiopians have a coffee grinding and brewing ritual that is every bit as complex and ceremonial as the better known Japanese tea ceremony.

Food scarcity is a major threat in much of the continent. Deserts are growing; droughts and famines are not rare. Western development aid, intended to increase agricultural yield, has often had the unintended effect of displacing native cultivars that have long since adapted to the challenging conditions of the African climate and that are often higher in nutritional value. In many parts of the continent, to be overweight signifies wealth and high social status, perhaps a reflection of the food insecurity faced by so much of the population.

At the same time, as in so much of the world, there is a widespread, strong sense of hospitality which involves offering food to visitors. If, as an outsider, one is able to visit a private dwelling, no matter how rudimentary, no matter how poor the hosts, one is likely to be fed well.

Perhaps no other part of the world is experiencing change more rapidly than is Africa. The expansion of cities and wage labor affect what and how the people eat. Western food ideas, western soft drinks, and western implements are ever more available, although food insecurity remains strongly present among the urban poor. However, cities bring all sorts of people together, often with interesting and diverse food traditions. For instance, there are strong South Asian influences, particularly in East Africa where Indians and Pakistanis were brought in by the British. And in the cosmopolitan centers like Capetown, most cuisines of the world are enjoyed.

Kola Nut
This caffeinated nut's first taste is bitter, but sweetens when chewed. It is enjoyed as a stimulant in many West African cultures, individually or in a group setting. The kola nut is used in popular beverages worldwide, namely Coca-Cola.

Edo Kola Nut Box
Made from wood and metal, this box is in the shape of a mud fish, which holds its tail in its mouth full of teeth. The sides of this piece are decorated, and the eyes are inlaid with metal. Museum object #AF2038

Peanuts

Not a nut at all, the peanut is a legume. It is a groundnut, closely related to the black-eyed pea. Peanuts originated in South America about 7,600 years ago. Peanut remains have been identified in ancient Incan burials. In the 16th century, the peanut was transported to Africa with Portuguese and Spanish traders and quickly took hold as a staple crop, especially in tropical West Africa as it grew well in this environment.

Images of peanuts are found among the unique metal weights displayed in the Penn Museum's Africa Gallery. These weights were made in the gold-rich regions of West Africa between the 15th and 19th centuries and take many forms: plant, animal, geometric, and human. Cast in bronze and used to weigh gold dust, they demonstrate the great wealth of the region at that time. The Asante reverence for the peanut is reflected in proverbs like: "Marriage is like a groundnut, you must crack it open to find what it contains."

Across Africa peanuts are eaten raw, roasted, boiled, salted, and stewed. Street vendors sell hot roasted peanuts in cones of rolled newspaper. Variations of peanut soups and stews are found in nearly every region, as is a pungent sauce for meats made with mashed peanuts, sautéed onion, garlic, vegetables, and spices. Peanuts are a common ingredient in salads and relishes and are served alongside rice and starches.

In the U.S. in the early 20th century, George Washington Carver of the Tuskegee Institute identified over 300 uses for the peanut. High in niacin, fiber, vitamin E, and several antioxidants, organizations like UNICEF and Doctors Without Borders feature peanut products in their campaigns to combat malnutrition among children.

Americans adore peanuts. In addition to using them as an ingredient, we eat them for snacks and add them to candies and cookies. And we love our peanut butter! Called "the pate of childhood" by food writer Florence Fabricant, the U.S. Peanut Council reports that Americans consume 1.5 billion pounds of peanut butter and other peanut products per year.

Moroccan Plate
In 1897–1898, Talcott Williams collected many beautiful ceramic bowls and plates for the Penn Museum. This piece contains a floral medallion in the center and is painted in blue, green, yellow, black, brown, and red. Museum object #29-201-134

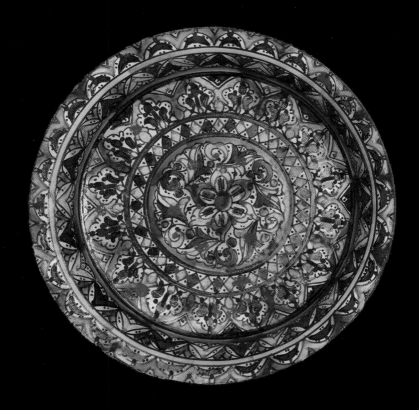

Artifact

MOROCCAN PLATE
Morocco
Late 19th century CE

Recipes

Peanut Soup

Spicy Stewed
Chicken Thighs

Beef Tagine
with Fruit
(pictured)

Savory Poached
Catfish

Parsleyed Jollof Rice

Cinnamon Yams

Plantain Chips

Braised Collard Greens

Spicy Red Cabbage
Slaw

Tapioca Coconut
Pudding

Peanut Soup

Peanuts are found in many African recipes, but nothing typifies the celebration of this humble groundnut better than peanut soup. Recipes for peanut soups and stews vary widely. This flavorful version is easy to prepare and hearty enough to stand as a main course.

Ingredients

2 tablespoons peanut oil

1 large white onion, sliced thin

1 tablespoon minced garlic

1 tablespoon minced ginger root

2 teaspoons cumin

2 teaspoons coriander

½ teaspoon cinnamon

Pinch ground cloves

Pinch cayenne

1 large tomato, peeled, seeded, and diced

2 large yams, peeled and diced

6 cups vegetable stock

1 cup roasted, shelled, unsalted peanuts

½ cup smooth peanut butter

Salt and pepper to taste

½ cup scallion greens, sliced very thin

Preparation

Serves 6-8

1. Heat oil in a stockpot or Dutch oven. Sauté onion 5-7 minutes, until lightly browned.
2. Add garlic, ginger, cumin, coriander, cinnamon, clove, and cayenne. Sauté 2 minutes.
3. Add tomatoes and yams. Sauté 2 minutes.
4. Add stock and peanuts. Bring to a boil. Reduce to a simmer. Cover and cook 30 minutes.
5. Turn off heat. Add peanut butter and purée the soup using an immersion blender.
6. Season with salt and pepper.
7. Serve garnished with sliced scallions.

Cinnamon

Cinnamon is scraped off in strips from the inner bark of certain trees, then rolled. Though bark from different trees might be described as cinnamon, "true" cinnamon from Sri Lanka is more aromatic and subtler than cassia from south China and Vietnam. Highly prized for its delicate flavor, as a preservative, as a component of incense, and in the embalming process, cinnamon costs 15 times as much as silver, according to Pliny, writing in the 1st century CE. Though its source was a mystery in the Middle Ages, it was probably brought by Arab traders through the Red Sea to Alexandria and then in Venetian ships to European markets.

Spicy Stewed Chicken Thighs

Referred to as Doro Wett *(with variations on spelling), there are many varieties of this traditional chicken stew. You could begin with a whole chicken and break down the parts, but thighs are most reliable. They cook evenly and remain juicy. Hard boiled eggs are always added at the end and are a surprising treat when taken with some of the spicy gravy and a bit of rice or lentils.*

Ingredients

1 large red onion, minced

½ teaspoon salt

¼ cup unsalted butter

½ teaspoon ground cardamom

¼ teaspoon ground black pepper

¼ teaspoon ground cloves

1 clove garlic, minced

2 tablespoons minced fresh ginger

1 tablespoon chili powder

2 cups chicken stock

4 pounds chicken thighs, bone in, skin on

1 lemon, juiced

3 eggs, hardboiled and peeled

3 cups prepared brown rice or braised lentils

Preparation

Serves 6

1. In a large pot over medium low heat, sauté onion and salt in butter until golden.
2. Add cardamom, pepper, cloves, garlic, ginger, and chili powder. Cook over low heat, stirring constantly for about 5 minutes.
3. Add stock and chicken thighs. Bring to a simmer and cook, partially covered, for 30 minutes.
4. Add lemon juice and hardboiled eggs. Bring to a boil. Reduce to simmer and cook, uncovered, 5 minutes.
5. Place brown rice or stewed lentils on a serving platter. Arrange chicken pieces on top.
6. Slice eggs in half lengthwise and arrange among chicken pieces.
7. Drench with sauce and serve.

Cardamom
Buy your cardamom (black, green, or white) in pods rather than ground for the best flavor. Use it in curries, to sweeten coffee as in Turkey, in pastries and breads as in Scandinavia, or chew it to sweeten the breath as did the ancient Egyptians. Its warm pungency lured first the Greeks and Romans and, beginning in the 16th century, European traders to the spice markets in Kerala in south India. Presently, Guatemala is the biggest producer of cardamom.

Beef Tagine with Fruit

North Africa is famous for its tagines, flavorful stews of chicken, lamb, or beef cooked in a lidded clay vessel called a tagine. *If you own one of these pretty creations, all the better, but any deep casserole or Dutch oven will do. This rendition is a beautiful meal in one. Lamb could be substituted successfully.*

Ingredients

1 tablespoon ground coriander

1 tablespoon ground cumin

1 tablespoon ground cinnamon

1 tablespoon ground ginger

1 tablespoon sweet paprika

1 tablespoon turmeric

1 teaspoon salt

½ teaspoon pepper

2 pounds stewing beef in 2 inch cubes

1 tablespoon olive oil

1 large onion, diced

1 small bunch cilantro, leaves and stalks separated

One 14-ounce can chickpeas, drained and rinsed

One 14-ounce can diced tomatoes, drained

2 tablespoons honey

3 cups vegetable stock

1 pound butternut squash, peeled, seeded, and cut into 2 inch cubes

4 ounces pitted prunes

4 ounces pitted dates

Preparation

Serves 4-6

1. Combine coriander, cumin, cinnamon, ginger, paprika, turmeric, salt, and pepper in a bowl large enough to hold the beef cubes.

2. Add the beef and massage the spice mixture into the meat. Cover with plastic wrap and refrigerate overnight.

3. Heat the olive oil in a tagine or Dutch oven until shimmering. Add the meat and brown well on all sides. Add the onion and cilantro stalks. Continue cooking until onions are softened and beginning to brown.

4. Add chickpeas, tomatoes, honey, and 2 cups of stock. Bring to a boil. Reduce to a simmer. Cover and simmer slowly for 1½ hours.

5. Remove lid, add squash, prunes, dates, and remaining stock. Bring to boil. Reduce to simmer. Cover and simmer slowly for 1½ hours.

6. Remove the lid and simmer 5-10 minutes to reduce the sauce, if necessary.

7. Transfer to a large serving bowl and garnish with reserved cilantro leaves.

Savory Poached Catfish

Here is a characteristic West African fish "stew." Catfish is a popular choice but any firm white fish fillet can be substituted. The thyme adds a surprising bright note to the fish and the sauce has a subtle depth that is a perfect complement to Parsleyed Jollof Rice.

Ingredients

1 teaspoon salt

1 teaspoon crushed dry thyme

2 tablespoons peanut oil

1 small red bell pepper, seeded and minced

½ teaspoon crushed red pepper flakes

One 6-ounce can tomato paste

1 medium onion, diced

1 clove garlic, minced

4 cups fish stock

Preparation
Serves 6

1. Season fish fillets with salt and thyme. Set aside.
2. Heat peanut oil in large skillet and sauté bell pepper, red pepper flakes, tomato paste, onion, and garlic for 2 minutes over medium heat.
3. Add stock. Bring to a boil, reduce to simmer, and cover.
4. Simmer over low heat for 30 minutes.
5. Gently place fish fillets into sauce and simmer for 10 minutes, partially covered.
6. Serve fillets over rice, sauced generously.

Parsleyed Jollof Rice

Recipes for Jollof Rice are as common across Africa as are variations of risotto in Italy. The main components are rice, tomato, and chilies. Palm oil is typically used and may be substituted here for a more healthful rendition. Some recipes call for the addition of chicken, fish, or seafood in addition to a variety of vegetables, resulting in a hearty main dish reminiscent of Jambalaya. This version is uncomplicated, straightforward, and flavorful. Brown rice is critical to the success of the dish, and, if a crust forms on the bottom, congratulations! That is often the prized morsel.

Ingredients

1½ cups cooked brown rice

1 large onion, diced

2 tablespoons vegetable oil

1 tablespoon tomato paste

1 green chili pepper, seeded and diced

1 cup vegetable stock

½ cup fresh parsley leaves, chopped

Preparation
Serves 4

1. Heat oil and sauté onion until soft and translucent.
2. Add tomato paste and chili. Sauté 2 minutes.
3. Add rice and stock. Bring to a boil.
4. Reduce heat, stir in parsley and simmer, uncovered, until all of the stock has evaporated.

Cinnamon Yams

Although some claim that yams and sweet potatoes are one in the same, the fact is that they are different tubers. Yams are native to the tropics and are a staple in Africa. Their bland, starchy flesh welcomes the hit of cinnamon and cayenne in this preparation. Do not skimp on the butter!

Ingredients

2 pounds yams, peeled and sliced into 1 inch thick rounds

½ teaspoon salt

1 clove garlic, peeled and smashed

1 ½ teaspoons cinnamon

¼ teaspoon cayenne pepper

¼ cup melted butter

¼ cup fresh chopped mint

Preparation

Serves 6

1. Place yams, salt, garlic, cinnamon, and cayenne in sauce pan. Add water just to cover. Bring to a boil.
2. Reduce to simmer. Cover and cook 15-20 minutes, until yams are tender.
3. Drain yams and arrange on serving platter.
4. Drizzle with butter and sprinkle with mint.

Plantain Chips

Plantain, the starchy cousin of the banana, is a frequent guest at an African meal. It is found fried, mashed, or even served as a dessert. It is perhaps most delicious when turned into a spicy version of potato chips! Great with a cold cola drink.

Ingredients

1 tablespoon cayenne pepper

2 teaspoons sea salt

Vegetable oil for frying

4 firm plantains, peeled and sliced into very thin rounds

Preparation

Serves 4-6

1. Place cayenne pepper and sea salt into a large paper bag and shake to combine.
2. Heat 3 inches oil in a deep pot or Dutch oven to 375 degrees.
3. Fry plantain slices in batches until crisp and golden.
4. Drain well on absorbent paper.
5. Place in bag with seasonings. Shake well and serve.

Plantains

Plantains are large, angular, and starchy, and are eaten cooked in contrast to dessert bananas, which are usually eaten raw and are smaller, more rounded, and sugary. Plantains are a staple food in tropical regions where they fruit all year round, making the crop a reliable food source in all seasons.

Braised Collard Greens

Vegetables, especially healthy dark greens, are a staple in African cuisine. Recipes often seem familiar to us, as they migrated to the Americas over the last several centuries. Here you could easily substitute kale or mustard greens, adjusting the amount of liquid and cooking time accordingly. The vinegar adds a bright note at the end. Use the best quality vinegar available.

Ingredients

1 pound fresh collard greens

1 tablespoon olive oil

1 large onion, diced

2 cloves garlic, minced

½ inch ginger, grated

1 large tomato, peeled, seeded, and diced

Vinegar for finishing

Preparation

Serves 4

1. Wash collard greens. Remove stems and center ribs. Tear into small pieces.
2. In a large saucepan, heat the oil and sauté onion until translucent.
3. Add garlic, ginger, and tomato. Sauté 1-2 minutes.
4. Add greens. Sauté 2 minutes.
5. Add just enough water to cover greens. Bring to boil.
6. Reduce to simmer. Cover and cook over medium low heat 20-30 minutes until collards are tender.
7. Drain any excess liquid. Serve with a generous drizzle of vinegar.

Cassava
Cassava, an edible starchy tuberous root, was brought to Africa from Brazil by Portuguese slave traders in the 16th century and then was transported to India and southeast Asia.

Spicy Red Cabbage Slaw

Here is variation of a summer picnic staple that will wake up your taste buds and become a go-to salad. Red cabbage stands up well to the zesty peanut dressing and looks quite pretty tossed with fresh sliced scallions.

Ingredients

¼ cup dry roasted unsalted peanuts, crushed fine

1 teaspoon fresh grated ginger

2 limes, zested and juiced

1 jalapeño or bird's eye chili, seeded and minced

¼ cup peanut oil

1 tablespoon honey

1 teaspoon salt

6 scallions, white and green parts sliced fine

1 medium red cabbage, sliced very thin

Preparation

Serves 6-8

1. Combine peanuts, ginger, lime zest, lime juice, jalapeño (or bird's eye chili), peanut oil, honey, and salt in the container of a blender or food processor and purée until very smooth.
2. Toss scallions and red cabbage together in a large bowl.
3. Pour dressing over cabbage mixture and mix thoroughly. Rest 30 minutes at room temperature before serving.

Tapioca Coconut Pudding

Tapioca is derived from the cassava root. Originally from the Americas, where it is known as yucca, cassava is a plentiful and common starch in the African diet. Here it appears in a familiar form but prepared with coconut. Feel free to add fresh pineapple or mango to this simple soothing dessert. This is also a lovely breakfast treat.

Ingredients

3 cups coconut milk

¼ cup instant tapioca

¼ cup sugar

¼ teaspoon salt

1 teaspoon vanilla

⅔ cup flaked coconut, toasted

1 cup heavy cream

Preparation

Serves 6

1. Combine coconut milk, tapioca, sugar, and salt in the top of a double boiler.
2. Cook the mixture over medium heat, stirring constantly, until tapioca pearls are completely transparent and pudding is thickened.
3. Remove from heat and stir in vanilla and toasted coconut.
5. To serve, spoon pudding into 6 individual bowls. Drizzle with cream. Serve warm or at room temperature.

Artifact

QING DYNASTY PAINTING

Canton, China

17th–19th century CE

The path to empire is through the stomachs of men—so said Confucius who maintained that proper diet, along with an army and trust, was essential to the founding of a successful state. Under Confucius, a strict set of dietary and ritual rules emerged that promoted hygiene and the proper handling of food. So respected were these regulations in ancient times that holy men were also masters of cookery. Indeed, in the 5th century BCE, Asian cuisine was elevated to a sacred art.

The wisdom of Confucius not only advanced principles of dietetic hygiene but also shaped the way modern Asian cooks approach food preparation. Use fresh, seasonal produce; maintain a clean workspace and utensils; cook thoroughly. Criteria established in the 5th century BCE were revolutionary at the time but appear sensible today and dramatically decrease disease. Hence the pride of sushi chefs in meticulously crafting their dishes. Thus modern standards for Asian cuisine reflect ancient values of honor and temperance.

Some ingredients in Asian cuisine are ubiquitous. Rice is a staple everywhere, and there are many kinds—long-grained, short-grained, sticky, jasmine, black, red, and purple. However, rice is a filler, so for people who are able to afford meat, it is no longer the centerpiece. Because the majority of the population, especially in Southeast Asia, are Buddhist, vegetables are eaten everywhere: cabbage (often pickled), soybeans, green beans, bamboo shoots, squashes, eggplants, leafy greens, cauliflowers, carrots, potatoes, leeks, mushrooms, radishes, garlic, and onions. No region in the world cooks vegetables as well.

Chinese cooking tends to be lightly spiced, using primarily soy sauce, scallions, ginger, garlic, and white pepper, except in the Hunan and Sichwan provinces, where chili peppers are added to most food, making it extremely spicy. A myth explains why so many famous

Artifact

FISH TRAY
Japan
ca. 19th century CE

Qing Dynasty Painting
The colors are still quite vivid in this page from a book depicting official Chinese costumes. It was painted on pith and paper and shows a well-dressed man being served tea by a servant. Museum object #17972

Fish Tray
This wooden tray is lacquered with images of five blue, rose, and gold fish and one prawn swimming among reeds, set against a black background. Museum object #CG94-1-108

revolutionaries came from these provinces—hot food makes for a fiery temperament. Other regions have their specialties: the best hams come from Yunnan; in Guangdong, goose and duck are favored; the Mongols in the north drink *kumiss* (fermented mares' milk); from Xinjiang come the best melons. Generally, rice is the main starch south of the Yangtse River and wheat noodles (symbols of longevity), north of it. China produces two-thirds of the world's pigs. Fish, chicken, guinea pigs, and ducks are also popular while sheep and beef are eaten mostly in the north and west. Many Chinese are lactose intolerant, so fermented milk products like yogurt, soy products, or tofu are preferred. Tea spread slowly from Burma and northeast India and was rare except in affluent houses until the 20th century.

Cooking implements include a wok, a stock pot, a steamer, a non-absorbent cutting board, and a sharp knife. Meals are served family style. Diners help themselves from common dishes placed in the middle of the table—approximately the same number of dishes as diners. An even number of dishes is considered lucky, and there should be a proper balance of vegetables, meats, and seafood. Vinegar is often mixed with sugar in sauces for stir-fries. Cornstarch is used as a thickener, even in scrambled eggs.

In Japan, a traditional meal is miso soup with three side dishes. Strictly vegetarian meals, the legacy of Buddhism, are rare today though meat, oils, fats, and dairy products are still eaten sparingly. Rice is the center of every meal although that custom too is giving way to western influences and alternatives like wheat or buckwheat noodles. Spices are used modestly, only ginger, soy sauce, and wasabi. Mushrooms are treasured, especially shiitake, but at least a dozen other varieties are also used in cooking. There is a formality to Japanese dining and food preparation. Special knives are required to cut fish, meat, and vegetables to enhance flavor and the proper transmission of heat. The appearance as well as the taste of food is valued. At a banquet, the order of courses is planned to contrast flavor, consistency, and color. A dish of raw fish might be followed by a grilled meat, then steamed vegetables, then crispy deep fried shrimp (tempura). Foods are served each in its own bowl and different flavors should not be mixed. Chopsticks must be held just so. Plates and bowls are placed according to custom and their colors often reflect the seasons.

Artifact

**CHINESE
SUGAR MOLD**
China
Date unknown

Chinese Sugar Mold
A rooster, bird, pyramid, and a geometric shape are all part of this wooden sugar mold. Museum object #89-13-261

Qing Dynasty Dish
Decorated with pink and green flowers, and a black and white bird, this porcelain dish may have been used for serving food. Small flowers and leaves decorate the yellow rim. Museum object #66-29-1

Artifact

QING DYNASTY DISH

China

19th century CE

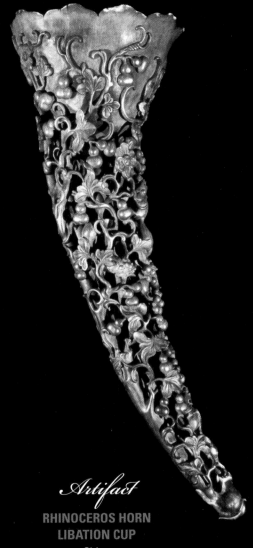

Artifact

**RHINOCEROS HORN
LIBATION CUP**

China

17th–19th century CE

No Korean meal is complete without rice served with *kimchi*, which is salted or pickled cabbage, radish, green onion, and cucumber, seasoned with red pepper flakes, chives, and garlic. As Korea is surrounded on three sides by sea, fish is a specialty along the coast. Inland, 70% of the land is mountainous resulting in a variety of natural produce and many provincial styles of cooking. Thus, along with the traditional bowls of rice or noodles and soup come a number of side dishes, sometimes up to 12, everything cut into bite-sized pieces, many pickled, salted, or fermented. All are served at the same time and placed in the center of the table. Soy products provide protein, but barbecued meat is increasingly popular. Chili peppers, originating in Central America and introduced into Japan by the Portuguese in the 17th century, along with other ingredients known all over Asia (soy sauce and paste, ginger, scallions, and sesame oil) are used for flavoring. Street food is popular in the cities (rice cakes, fish cakes, and ramen noodles with fish or meat). Although Korea has suffered politically from its proximity to China and Japan, gastronomically, it has benefitted.

Southeast Asian food is especially rich and varied and is considered some of the world's healthiest. Oil is used sparingly. Attention is paid to balance: sour, sweet, salty, and bitter tastes must be part of every meal. Dishes must be colorful. Spicy foods are served with cooling sauces. Coconut milk supplies the liquid for curries. Spices are stronger, more aromatic, than in other parts of Asia. Soy sauce, fish sauce (from fermented fish), turmeric, lemon grass, ginger, cinnamon, coriander, cilantro, chili peppers and pastes, tamarind, and lime juice are used liberally. Foreign traders were attracted to the area, initially for its fabulous spices: Chinese in the 7th century and Arabs in the 11th century each brought their favorite foods. From India came curries. From Holland, with the Dutch East India Company merchants, came bread, meat, and butter. The surrounding seas are rich in fish and shellfish. Westerners are sometimes surprised by some of the more exotic indigenous foods of the area: fertilized duck eggs complete with embryo, silk worms, dog, snake, soft shell turtle, mouse, cobra, pig brains—and the durian fruit, which has been described as smelling like a combination of pig excrement and turpentine, garnished with a gym sock, but also as surpassing in exquisite flavor all other fruits in the world. All Asian food is an adventure for Westerners, but in Southeast Asia it is both a delight and a challenge!

Artifact

BRONZE DING
China
Western Zhou Dynasty
1046–771 BCE

Rhinoceros Horn Libation Cup
Squirrels and grapes, popular designs in both the Ming and Qing Dynasties, are deeply carved on this large rhinoceros horn libation cup. Rhino horn has been described as an aphrodisiac, and squirrels and grapes were connected with reproduction. Museum object #7556

Bronze Ding
This ritual vessel has a cover that is ornamented with wide-mouthed spiral-horned animals in high relief. Aside from its decorative appeal, the cover would have kept food warm when used as a serving dish. Museum object #41-25-1A, B

Rice

Rice is a member of the grass family. Some think that it was first domesticated in China's Pearl River Valley *ca*. 11,000 BCE; others, that its origin was in southern India *ca*. 7000 BCE. Regardless, the production and consumption of rice spread throughout South and Southeast Asia as a staple grain by the 6th century BCE. Trade took it to western Asia and Europe as early as the 2nd century CE and to the New World with the Europeans by the 15th century CE.

Rice is now consumed worldwide and is second only to maize in tons produced. It thrives where the climate is warm and wet. While large scale producers employ advanced technologies for planting and harvesting, small growers often cultivate by hand. The dozens of varieties of rice are classified according to grain length: short, medium, or long. Short varieties tend to be sticky and are favored in Japan where they are critical in dishes like sushi. Medium grained rice absorbs liquids and is used in the risottos of Italy and the paellas of Spain. People across much of Southeast Asia prefer delicately flavored long-grain jasmine rice that produces fluffy mounds.

In the 6th century BCE, Confucius, an epicure as well as a philosopher, advocated strict rules about food preparation and service. He demanded that his rice be polished white. Thus, white rice became the norm. Preparations can be elaborate, such as Chinese Eight Treasures Rice, perfectly white rice decorated with colorful fruits, nuts, and seeds, and served at New Year celebrations. Ordinarily, a simple bowl of steaming white rice accompanies every meal.

Rice wine and rice vinegar are used to preserve other foods. Rice paper is a medium for artists. Spring rolls are bundled in rice-based wonton wrappers. Gluten-free rice flour appears in 21st century recipes, and we are rediscovering the delightful flavors and textures of less processed rice. No less beautiful, these brown, red, or black varieties bring color as well as improved nutrition to your table.

Korean Traveling Dining Kit
Utensils—including chopsticks, spoons, forks, a knife, and tweezers—are included in this portable dining kit. Those objects, along with two metal cups, can be packed away in the cylindrical metal container with red cord tassels. Museum object #64-1-5

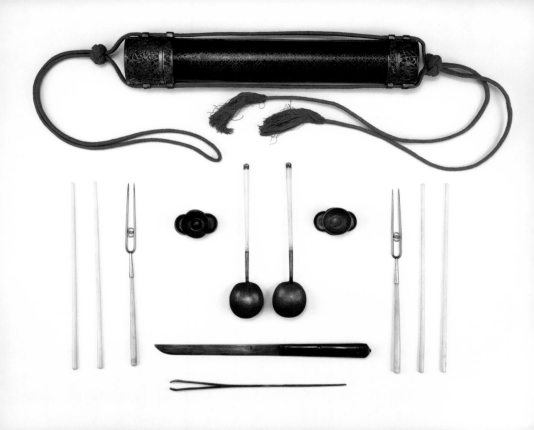

Shrimp and Cilantro Spring Rolls

Across Asia we find foods cooked or served in wrappers, eliminating the need for utensils. Perhaps there is a no more recognizable Asian finger food than the spring roll. These lovely crisp packets make a perfect starter. Serve them with our tangy Soy Dipping Sauce.

Ingredients

1 dozen large shrimp, cooked and peeled

1 medium carrot, peeled and finely grated

½ cup cilantro leaves, chopped fine

2 tablespoons scallion greens, chopped fine

1 tablespoon finely grated ginger

1 egg white, beaten

1 tablespoon lime zest

1 dozen spring roll wrappers

Peanut oil for frying

Preparation

Serves 6 as an appetizer

1. Purée six shrimp in a food processer. Mince the remaining six shrimp.
2. Combine the shrimp, carrot, cilantro, scallion, ginger, egg white, and lime zest.
3. Place spring roll wrappers on clean work surface and top each with a rounded tablespoon of filling.
4. Fold sides over filling and roll from front to back forming a snug package.
5. Heat about 1 inch peanut oil in a skillet over medium heat. Brown spring rolls on all sides.
6. Drain and serve with Soy Dipping Sauce.

Soy Dipping Sauce

Ingredients

⅛ cup water

½ cup soy sauce

2 tablespoons Chinese black vinegar

1 tablespoon apricot jam

1 small red chili, minced

Preparation

Yield ¾ cup

1. Combine all ingredients until jam is dissolved.
2. Serve with Shrimp and Cilantro Spring Rolls and Marbled Tea eggs.

Marbled Tea Eggs

Found on menus dating back as far as the time of Confucius, Marbled Tea Eggs are a beautiful, sweet/spicy accompaniment for very cold sake.

Ingredients

1 dozen eggs

⅓ cup soy sauce

½ cup very strong brewed black tea

1 star anise

1 stick cinnamon

1 tablespoon brown sugar

Preparation

Serves 6 as an appetizer

1. Place eggs in large saucepan. Cover with cold water. Bring to full boil. Cover and remove from heat. Let stand 12 minutes.
2. Remove eggs to an ice water bath. Retain water from boiling.
3. Return water in pot to boiling.
4. Add soy, tea, anise, cinnamon, and brown sugar. Boil 5 minutes, uncovered.
5. Remove eggs from ice bath and gently roll on counter top to crack shells all over. Do not peel.
6. Place eggs in a tall, lidded container and strain tea mixture over to cover completely.
7. Cool to room temperature, seal the container and refrigerate 3-5 days.
8. Remove eggs from liquid, peel, and serve whole with Soy Dipping Sauce.

Crab and Noodle Soup

Noodles are as common in Asian cuisine as they are in Italian cooking. In fact, it is believed that Marco Polo introduced the noodle to his benefactors upon his return from his journey to the East. This light quick soup is as delicious as it is beautiful and will work equally well as a first course or as an entrée.

Ingredients

One 6-ounce package medium sized rice noodles

2 baby bok choy

1 tablespoon butter

1 tablespoon grated fresh ginger

2 cups fish stock

½ cup coconut milk

¾ pound lump crab meat

1 tablespoon rice wine

1 tablespoon fish sauce

¼ teaspoon ground white pepper

4 scallions, sliced thin

Preparation

Serves 4

1. Prepare noodles according to package directions. Rinse and set aside.
2. Trim away the base and remove any tough outer leaves of each head of bok choy. Separate into individual leaves. Slice lengthwise into thin strips. Set aside.
3. Melt butter in large saucepan over medium heat and sauté ginger 1 minute.
4. Add stock and water. Bring to a boil.
5. Add coconut milk and crab. Simmer on low 2-3 minutes.
6. Add bok choy, rice wine, fish sauce, pepper, and scallions. Bring to a quick boil.
7. Divide noodles among 4 bowls and pour soup over noodles. Serve.

Lions Head Meatballs with Napa Cabbage

Meatballs and cabbage are found in northern European and Mediterranean, as well as Asian cuisines. In this rendition, the meatball represents the "lion's head" and the cabbage is his mane. Lions are revered as symbols of strength in many cultures, and especially among the Chinese. This traditional dish is enhanced by the use of Szechuan pepper, so try not to substitute.

Ingredients

1½ pounds ground pork

½ pound ground beef

½ pound shiitake mushrooms, minced

6 garlic cloves, minced

1 inch ginger, peeled and grated

¼ cup tamari sauce

1 egg, lightly beaten

1 teaspoon ground Szechuan pepper

½ cup cornstarch

1 cup chicken stock

1 medium head napa cabbage, julienned

Peanut oil for frying

Preparation

Serves 6-8

1. Heat 2 tablespoons oil in a large lidded skillet and sauté mushrooms, garlic, and ginger 3-4 minutes until softened.

2. In a large bowl, combine meats, mushrooms, garlic, ginger, tamari sauce, egg, and pepper.

3. Form 12 large meatballs. Coat thoroughly with cornstarch.

4. Heat 1 inch oil in wok or large skillet until shimmering. Fry meatballs until browned on all sides. Remove and drain.

5. Pour off fat in skillet and wipe inside with paper towel. Add stock and bring to a simmer.

6. Add ½ cabbage, then meatballs, then remaining cabbage. Bring to a boil, cover, and reduce to a simmer.

7. Simmer 10-15 minutes until cabbage in crisp tender.

8. Uncover and simmer 3-5 minutes more to reduce sauce. Serve.

Shiitake Mushrooms

Mushrooms have been gathered from dead wood in the forests of China and Japan for over 2,000 years. In Japanese, "shii" means "from a hardwood tree," and "take" means "mushroom." Since the 1980s, shiitake production has become a global industry with local farms in most western countries in addition to large scale importation from China, Japan, Korea, and elsewhere.

Sweet and Sour Bass Fillets

Asian cooking often offers contrasts of flavor and texture. Here the tangy vinegars and salty tamari sauce play against the brown sugar. Crisp carrots and water chestnuts balance the delicate shiitake mushrooms and bass. The pleasing result will satisfy all of your taste buds.

Ingredients

Peanut oil for frying

1 clove garlic, minced

4 scallions, sliced thin

6 large shiitake mushrooms, sliced

¼ cup grated carrot

¼ cup thinly sliced water chestnuts

2 tablespoons brown sugar

1 tablespoon freshly grated ginger

1 tablespoon rice vinegar

1 tablespoon shanxi vinegar

2 tablespoons tamari sauce

1 tablespoon corn starch

1 cup chicken broth at room temperature

4 large bass fillets, skin removed

3 tablespoons flour

Preparation

Serves 4

1. Heat 2 tablespoons peanut oil in large skillet and sauté garlic, scallions, mushrooms, carrot, and water chestnuts for 2 minutes, stirring constantly.

2. Add brown sugar, ginger, vinegars, and tamari. Simmer 2 minutes, stirring constantly. Lower heat.

3. In a small bowl, whisk cornstarch into broth. Slowly stir broth mixture into vegetables and simmer until thickened. Remove from heat.

4. Dust fillets with flour to coat lightly.

5. Heat ¼ inch oil in a frying pan large enough to hold filets.

6. Fry fillets until golden, about 5 minutes per side.

7. Transfer fillets to vegetable sauce. Swirl to coat. Serve.

Water Chestnut
The water chestnut is not a nut at all, but an aquatic vegetable that grows in marshes, underwater in the mud. The plant has tube-shaped, leafless green stems growing above the mud. The small, rounded corms (underground bulbs) have a crisp white flesh and can be eaten raw, slightly boiled, or grilled, and are often pickled or canned.

Gingered Tofu and Asparagus Stir Fry

Tofu, technically coagulated soy milk, probably originated in China about 2,000 years ago. Favored as a vegetarian protein source by East Asian Buddhists, it traveled to East and Southeast Asia where it is found in dozens of varieties from silken to extra firm. Firm varieties work especially well as meat substitutes and are easily flavored with marinades. Here is an especially beautiful and delicious example.

Ingredients

2 tablespoons peanut oil

2 tablespoons sugar

4 tablespoons rice vinegar

4 tablespoons soy sauce

2 tablespoons grated fresh ginger

1 tablespoon Chinese chili sauce

1 pound extra-firm tofu, drained and cut into 1 inch cubes

1 pound young asparagus spears

½ pound baby bok choy, sliced thin

1 carrot, grated

2 tablespoons sesame oil

2 cups jasmine rice, prepared according to package directions

Preparation

Serves 6

1. Combine peanut oil, sugar, vinegar, soy sauce, ginger, and chili sauce in a shallow bowl.
2. Add tofu and cover. Refrigerate 2 hours.
3. Remove tofu from marinade. Reserve marinade.
4. Remove woody lower portions from asparagus and slice diagonally into 1½ inch pieces.
5. In large skillet or wok, heat sesame oil over medium high.
6. Add tofu, asparagus, bok choy, and carrot. Sauté, stirring constantly for 2 minutes.
7. Add reserved marinade and cook about 2 minutes, until asparagus and bok choy are crisp tender.
8. Serve over jasmine rice.

Soy Beans
Soy beans were domesticated first in China and are excellent substitutes for animal products, as they are high in protein. Known for its versatility, soy is used to make milk, tofu, yogurt, cheese, oil, and flour. Soy products are believed to reduce the risk of cancer and heart disease. As the plant dies and decays, it returns nitrogen to the soil in which it grows.

Julian's Red Curry Chicken

Curry dishes have been a feature of Asian cuisine for thousands of years. Probably originating in the Indus Valley, these highly spiced preparations for meats and vegetables likely migrated with Buddhist monks as they traveled east during the 7th century. Curries can be dry or wet, red or green, hot or mild. Regional variations abound. Don't mistake the bright yellow curry powder commonly found in your local grocery store for the real thing. It is a weak commercial imitation originally packaged for the English homemaker in the 19th century. You will understand the difference once you have prepared this dish. Reminiscent of its Indian origins, it is hot, spicy, and luscious.

Ingredients

1 teaspoon cumin seeds

1 teaspoon coriander seeds

7 whole cloves

1 teaspoon cardamom seeds

3 tablespoons canola oil

1 medium onion, diced

3 cloves garlic, minced

2 inches fresh ginger, peeled and grated

1 green Thai chili, diced

1 teaspoon cinnamon

1 teaspoon ground turmeric

1 tablespoon red curry paste
(hot or mild, to taste)

2 pounds boneless, skinless chicken
thighs or legs, cut into 1½ inch pieces

3 tablespoons tomato paste

1 cup chicken stock

Pinch salt

½ cup chopped fresh cilantro

2 cups white rice prepared according
to package directions

Preparation

Serves 4

1. In a small skillet, dry toast cumin and coriander seeds over medium heat until fragrant, about 1-2 minutes.

2. Place cumin seeds, coriander seeds, cloves, and cardamom seeds in a spice or coffee grinder and grind to a fine powder.

3. Heat canola oil in a large skillet until shimmering. Add onion and sauté over medium heat until soft and translucent.

4. Lower heat and add freshly ground spices, garlic, ginger, Thai chili, cinnamon, turmeric, and red curry paste to skillet and cook, stirring, for 5 minutes.

5. Raise the heat to medium. Add the chicken. Stir 5-8 minutes until the chicken is lightly browned and coated with spice mixture on all sides.

6. Add the tomato paste, stock, and salt. Bring to a boil, reduce to a simmer, and cook, partially covered, for 20-30 minutes, until chicken is tender. Add additional water or stock if the sauce becomes too thick.

7. Transfer to a serving platter, garnish with cilantro, and serve with steaming rice.

Ginger
Ginger or ginger root is a rhizome: a root or shoot that grows underground from nodes on the subterranean plant. It grows widely from Jamaica to Nigeria to India. The Romans used it to counteract acidity and to disguise the taste of decaying food. The Chinese used it as a stimulant. It was given to new mothers to restore their strength. Ginger is common in Asian and Indian cooking and may have anti-inflammatory properties.

Snow Pea and Shiitake Stir Fry

Originating in South China, the wok has been a go-to cooking tool in East and Southeast Asian cuisine for centuries. While often associated with quick, high temperature stir fry preparations, as seen here, it might be used for boiling, steaming, or even stewing. The success of this made-in-minutes dish depends on having all ingredients prepared and assembled before the oil is heated.

Ingredients

1 tablespoon sesame oil

2 cloves garlic, minced

1 inch fresh ginger, grated

1 small red chili, seeded and sliced fine

½ pound snow peas

½ pound shiitake mushrooms, sliced thin

1 tablespoon fish sauce

1 teaspoon soy sauce

1 tablespoon sesame seeds

Preparation   Serves 4

1. Heat oil in wok or large skillet over medium high heat.
2. Add garlic, ginger, and chili and stir fry 2 minutes.
3. Add snow peas and stir fry 3 minutes or until crisp tender.
4. Add mushrooms and stir fry 1 minute, just until softened and some juices are released.
5. Remove from heat and stir in fish sauce and soy sauce. Distribute evenly.
6. Transfer to a serving dish and garnish with sesame seeds.

Cucumber Cashew Salad

The best salads are often the simplest combinations of a few well paired ingredients. Here cool crunchy cucumbers and salty meaty cashews are married in a subtle sweet sour dressing.

Ingredients

3 medium cucumbers, peeled

2 tablespoons rice vinegar

2 teaspoons sugar

1 tablespoon Chinese chili sauce

1 large shallot, sliced very thin

½ cup cilantro leaves, whole

1 cup toasted cashews, chopped

1 tablespoon fish sauce

Preparation   Serves 6

1. Slice cucumber in half lengthwise. Scoop out seeds. Cut into ¼ inch slices.
2. Mix vinegar, sugar, and chili sauce until well combined.
3. Add cucumbers, shallot, and cilantro. Toss and chill 1 hour.
4. To serve, add cashews and fish sauce. Toss well.

Artifact

COARSE GRAIN BREAD
Dra Abu El-Naga, Egypt
1292–1190 BCE

Egypt

No other place in the world sits at the intersection of three continents. Egypt, like the nearby Levant, has been a crossroads through which people, ideas, and foods have flowed through the ages, influenced by and influencing Africa, Asia, and Europe. As one of the earliest and most enduring of urban civilizations, the population of ancient Egypt required large supplies of food to support the building of the pyramids and other monumental structures in a dry desert environment.

The regular flooding of the Nile River provided an abundance of Egyptian grain. Rich volcanic soils of the Ethiopian highlands were regularly deposited onto the waiting fields of Egyptian farmers alongside the river and in the highly fertile Nile Delta. Even today, as you fly over the Nile Valley, you see a very narrow ribbon of green on either side of the river, edged on both sides by the golden desert stretching to the far distance.

Dependent upon rainfall to the south, the annual Nile flood was also a potential menace. Over-flooding could and did devastate farmlands; light rainfall could lead to prolonged drought. Partly to solve these problems, the Aswan High Dam was constructed in the late 1960s and completed in 1970. For the first time, the flooding was under human control. This allowed for thousands of new hectares to fall under irrigation, both for food crops and for the economically important cotton crop. The huge Lake Nasser formed behind the dam spawned a new fishing industry, albeit one quite far from the fish-eating market. New fish processing factories responded to this condition. However, controlling the Nile flood has also had some unwelcome effects. Less silt flowing downstream has led to erosion in the Delta, and changes in the mineral content of the water that flows through the Dam has increased the salinity of downstream soils.

Egypt's cultural and gustatory continuity is matched only by that of China. Just as the pyramids have survived, so have many of the ancient foods that were consumed for millennia. Among the oldest are pulses, especially fava and lentil, which go back at least 8,000 years. Wheat has similar antiquity, originating in either Anatolia or Mesopotamia. Bread-making and beer-brewing, related activities, are documented on early Egyptian tomb walls.

Coarse Grain Bread
Small, conical pieces of bread, each about six centimeters or over two inches long, were recovered from Pyramid 4 at Dra Abu El-Naga, Egypt. They are made from coarse grain with the husk mixed in. Museum object #29-87-561

Figs, dates, and pomegranates appear on depictions of offering tables or in the shape of ornaments. Cattle and sheep keeping—for milk and meat—are equally ancient. The tilapia, known as "Nile perch" and eaten just about everywhere, has been swimming in the Nile since before the earliest human presence. Other fish species are also consumed.

The ancient Egyptians did us the favor of portraying much about farming, cooking, and eating in the wall decorations that abound in temples and tombs, and in food offerings found preserved in burials. Hence, we know what foods were consumed, how they were grown and prepared, and how and which animals were butchered. We can also get a sense of which foodstuffs and foodways date from the times of the Pharaohs, and which are the result of later Arab and European influences.

Included among the treasures that Howard Carter found in the tomb of Tutankhamun were boxes and pottery vessels containing wheat, barley, chick peas, lentils, garlic, coriander, cumin, and sesame. Ingredients for beer-making were found in addition to wine vessels. Among the fruits were dates, dried grapes, *dom palm* fruit, *persea*, and the seeds of watermelon. The Pharaoh also took with him into his next life containers of honey, various breads, and cuts of oxen, sheep, goats, ducks, and geese. Eternity is a long time; the young king wanted to be prepared.

Thanks to the ancient Egyptian desire to document their lives, and to the persistence of a literary tradition going back thousands of years, we know quite a bit about Egyptian beliefs as well as practices. Onions were thought to have curative and magical properties, and some deities may have been given onions as an offering. Onions probably originated to the east, perhaps in India. Ancient Egyptian farmers developed their own varieties, along with leeks and garlic. Onions were considered poor peoples' food; the workers who built the Pyramids were said to have been fueled by bread, beer, and onions. At the same time, onions were inserted into the eye sockets of pharaohs to fill the area left by shrunken eyeballs.

One would be hard pressed to find another land where today one food so predominates as does the fava bean in Egypt. *Fuul*, the paste, stew, or soup made from the fava comes

Artifact

NILE FISH AMULET
Hu, Egypt
Middle Kingdom
1938–1759 BCE

Nile Fish Amulet
The two halves of this pendant of a catfish are molded around a core, with the details of the fish engraved into the metal itself. Fish were not only a staple of the Egyptian diet, but some species of fish, including the lepidotus and the tilapia, also had religious symbolism for the ancient Egyptians. Museum object #E3989

Gourd Vessel
This realistic green faience rhyton with black markings is from Tomb 2010 at Sedment. It represents a vegetable, probably a squash or a cucumber. Museum object #E15436

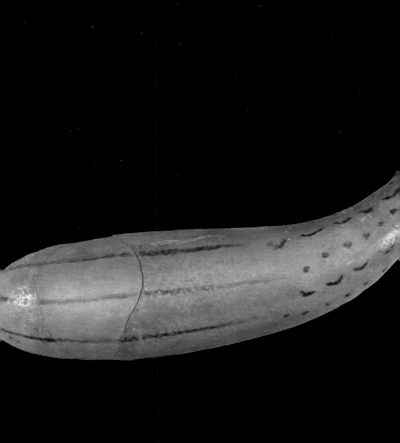

Artifact

GOURD VESSEL
Sedment, Egypt
1292–1075 BCE

Artifact

TOMB CHAPEL OF KA(I)PURA

Saqqara, Egypt

2415–2298 BCE

in a wide assortment of styles, depending on what is mixed into it or served on top. Herbs, spices, tomatoes, eggs, nuts, almost anything can be added, and fuul is found everywhere. Egyptians will argue about where the best fuul is made. The fava plant is an outstanding performer, easy to grow, extremely hardy, drought resistant, able to survive in a wide range of climates, and when it decays, the plant adds nitrogen to the soil.

Egyptians eat stews, dips, and soups from other pulses such as lentils and chickpeas. While some, particularly the brown lentil, may be originally Egyptian, others, and the manner in which they are prepared, may have spread from the east as Arabian peoples moved across North Africa in the 7th and 8th centuries. These crops are also easy to grow and high in protein. Chickpea hummus, ground roasted eggplant dishes, olives, and flat breads, which are the stuff of *mezze* courses throughout the Middle East, are also served in Egyptian homes and restaurants.

In ancient times, meat, principally from cattle, sheep, and fowl, and less often from pigs (even pre-Islam), was primarily the food of the elite. We find scenes of animals being presented to the pharaohs, of the animals' slaughter, and of the serving of great piles of meats. When ordinary people had meat, it was usually as a garnish for an otherwise largely vegetarian diet, a diet that was followed for economic reasons. In contemporary Egypt, meats are often grilled on skewers, as is common around the Mediterranean and across Asia into India—small chunks of meat alternating with pieces of vegetables cooked over a fire.

Fish, on the other hand, was, and still is, far more widely consumed, particularly along the Nile and in coastal regions. The tilapia is generally broiled, baked, or fried, and often served with lemons. One of the most evocative sights in Egypt today is the triangular-sailed *felucca* as they ply the Nile with net booms, sweeping up thousands of these small perch.

Present-day Egyptians have a taste for sweets, including *baklava*, which is found throughout the Middle East: phyllo pastry layered with crushed nuts (pistachios, almonds, or pignolas) steeped in honey or sugar syrup. Another favorite is *halva*, a confection made with semolina flour, sesame paste (*ca*), dried dates, and other fruits, and, once again, sweet syrup. Fruit—bananas, peaches, apricots, grapes, figs, and mulberries—is often eaten at the end of a meal, as fruit grows well in the fertile valley of the Nile.

Tomb Chapel of Ka(i)pura
Carved and painted scenes decorate the west wall and corridor of the tomb chapel of Ka(i)pura. Here, we see a small section that shows food offerings to the deceased above a series of offering bearers. Museum object #E15729

Meroitic Jar
This ceramic jar was found in a tomb in Nubia, Egypt's neighbor to the south. It is painted with a frieze of foraging giraffes and undulating snakes spitting ankh signs. Museum object #E8183

Tilapia

The ancient Egyptians held the tilapia, a fast-growing fresh water fish, in high esteem. A symbol of the power of fertility and regeneration, amulets shaped like tilapia were popular in ancient Egypt. Tilapia decorated serving bowls and appeared in wall paintings. Female tilapia are known to carry their newborn in their mouths for protection. The Penn Museum's charming, plump, tilapia-shaped rattle may be a reference to this maternal practice. Or the rattle may have simply had a musical function in a religious setting. Egyptians created a number of different fish hieroglyphs, including one that represented the tilapia.

A pre-dynastic stone palette from 3000 BCE is thought to contain the earliest image of this fish. The walls of an Egyptian tomb from 2000 BCE are decorated with a bas-relief illustrating perhaps the earliest large-scale aquaculture: tilapia held in closed shallow ponds along the banks of the Nile. Ancient Egyptians took advantage of the tilapia's tolerance for close quarters and its reproductive prowess to produce a ready source of protein. Irrigation kept ponds fresh, and captive fish were easily harvested. The same practice continues today in tanks or cages rather than ponds. Worldwide tilapia production, entirely farmed, is equal in value to that of salmon and trout. Because it feeds on algae and plants, this fish is also inexpensive to cultivate. Egypt is the second largest producer of tilapia, and it is not uncommon for the morning's harvest from fish farms along the northern Nile to appear on Cairo menus at lunchtime as the "catch of the day."

Tilapia is an inexpensive low-fat, mild, white fish. Whole or filleted, it can be baked, stuffed, broiled, pan-seared, blackened, crusted, or fried. Tilapia is an economical stand-in for catfish, flounder, or striped bass. It is most often used in the fish stews common to much of Egypt and North Africa. So ubiquitous is the tilapia in Egyptian culture that traditional family recipes simply call for "fish," assuming tilapia.

Tilapia Rattle
This green faience fish rattle may have been used as a musical instrument. In ancient Egypt, the tilapia was symbolic of birth and regeneration and also decorated bowls and other objects. Museum object #E13005

Artifact

TILAPIA RATTLE
Egypt
Date unknown

Recipes

Lentil Spread

Tabbouleh

Pickled Pearl Onions
(pictured)

Crisp Flatbread

Sesame Mangoes

Herb Stuffed Tilapia
with Cinnamon Rice

Koshari
Lentil, Rice, Macaroni
and Chickpea
Casserole

Fresh Fava Salad

Sweet and Sour Okra

Fig and Walnut Pastry

Lentil Spread

Lentils were grown in the ancient world for thousands of years, eventually making their way into Asian, Mediterranean, European, and African cuisines. Brown lentils, sometimes called Egyptian lentils, are the most common variety. Their soft texture and mild flavor make them a perfect vehicle for this surprisingly luscious and nutritious version of hummus.

Ingredients

1 cup brown lentils

⅓ cup minced carrot

⅓ cup minced onion

⅓ cup minced celery

2 tablespoons minced garlic, total

5 tablespoons olive oil, total

4 fresh sage leaves

5 cups cold water

1 teaspoon salt

½ teaspoon black pepper

½ cup minced fresh parsley, total

Preparation

Serves 8-10 as an appetizer

1. Bring lentils, carrot, onion, celery, 1 tablespoon garlic, 2 tablespoons olive oil, sage, and water to a boil. Reduce to a simmer and cook, uncovered, until lentils and vegetables are very tender, about 40-50 minutes.
2. Drain lentil mixture, remove sage leaves, and purée in food processer.
3. Add salt, pepper, remaining garlic, and 2 tablespoons oil. Process until very smooth.
4. Adjust seasoning, stir in ¼ cup parsley. Cool to room temperature.
5. To serve, drizzle with remaining olive oil and sprinkle with remaining parsley.

Tabbouleh

Bulgur is one of the earliest "processed foods." Wheat berries are cooked, hulled, and dried, producing this nutty and nutritious grain that softens easily. Wheat, in all its variations, was plentiful in Egypt and is known to have been produced in the Nile River Valley at least 6,000 years ago.

Ingredients

1 cup quick cooking bulgur wheat

2 tomatoes, peeled, seeded, and chopped fine

1 bunch mint, chopped fine (about 1 cup)

2 large shallots, minced

1 small cucumber, peeled, seeded, and chopped fine

1 tablespoon sesame oil

2 tablespoons olive oil

¼ cup lemon juice

1 teaspoon salt

1 pinch cayenne pepper

Preparation

Serves 6

1. In a medium bowl, cover bulgur with boiling water. Let stand, covered, 60 minutes until plump. Drain thoroughly to remove all water.
2. Combine bulgur with remaining ingredients. Chill 1 hour before serving.

Pickled Pearl Onions

Egyptians frequently preserve fruits or vegetables by pickling, and offer them at most meals, even breakfast! Onions were highly valued by ancient Egyptians and their residue has been identified with the burial remains of pharaohs. Pearl onions hold up well in pickling and may be closest to those described as being like white teeth in Old Kingdom texts.

Ingredients

2 cups fresh pearl onions, peeled

1 bay leaf, crumbled

8 sprigs fresh thyme

4 sprigs fresh mint

2 garlic cloves, sliced thin

⅔ cup water

⅔ cup wine vinegar

¼ cup sugar

2 teaspoons salt

1 teaspoon coriander seed

1 teaspoon black peppercorns

1 teaspoon mustard seed

Preparation

1. Blanch onions in a large pot of boiling water, 3-4 minutes, until just tender. Drain and place in an ice water bath.
2. Layer cooled onions with bay leaf, thyme, mint, and garlic in a 1 pint container such as a Mason jar.
3. In a medium saucepan, bring water, vinegar, sugar, salt, coriander seed, peppercorns, and mustard seed to a boil. Reduce to a simmer and cook until sugar is dissolved.
4. Pour hot liquid into jar, covering onions completely. Cool, uncovered, at room temperature. Seal and refrigerate up to 2 weeks.

Yield 1 pint

Onions
Onions are said to have been introduced to Greece from Egypt by Alexander the Great, in order to bring courage to his troops. This vegetable is now grown and eaten throughout the world. Onions contain similar chemical compounds as garlic and have potential anti-inflammatory, anti-cholesterol, and antioxidant properties.

Crisp Flatbread

This simple bread preparation yields thin cracker-like loaves similar to those found throughout Egypt. Break the finished product into large pieces for scooping hummus or tabbouleh.

Ingredients

1 cup warm water

1 package dry yeast

¼ cup butter, melted and cooled

1 ½ teaspoons salt

¼ teaspoon sugar

3 ½ cups all purpose flour

Preparation

Yields 4 loaves

1. Combine water and yeast in a large bowl. Allow yeast to proof, 10-15 minutes.
2. Add butter, salt, sugar, and 2 cups flour. Combine until smooth.
3. Stir in additional flour, ½ cup at a time, until dough is stiff.
4. Turn dough onto floured surface and knead 10 minutes.
5. Place dough in a large buttered bowl. Cover with plastic wrap and let rise until doubled in bulk.
6. Preheat oven to 350 degrees.
7. Punch down dough and knead 1 minute on a floured board.
8. Divide dough into 4 pieces. Roll each into a rectangle slightly smaller than a standard baking sheet.
9. Place one loaf on a baking sheet and bake 20-25 minutes until blistered and golden brown. Repeat as oven capacity permits.
10. Cool loaves thoroughly before serving.

Sesame Mangoes

Mangoes were probably brought into East Africa from India centuries ago. Now they are a common ingredient in Egyptian desserts, preserves, and chutneys. Here is a savory accompaniment for grilled fish or game that is simple to prepare and lovely to look at.

Ingredients

2 tablespoons peanut oil

1 large red onion, diced

2 garlic cloves, minced

1 tablespoon grated fresh ginger

1 small green chili, seeded and minced

Pinch chili powder

2 large mangoes, diced

2 tablespoons sesame seeds

¼ cup chopped fresh mint

1 teaspoon sesame oil

Preparation

Serves 6 as a condiment

1. Heat peanut oil in large skillet and sauté onions until transparent.
2. Add garlic, ginger, chili, chili powder, and cook over low heat 5 minutes. Remove from heat and cool.
3. Transfer mixture to a bowl. Add mangoes, sesame seeds, mint, and sesame oil. Stir to combine.

Herb Stuffed Tilapia with Cinnamon Rice

Tilapia may be one of the earliest farmed fish, raised in Nile tributaries by ancient Egyptians. Here, the mild flavor of the tilapia is enhanced by herbs and spices and paired with traditional creamy cinnamon rice.

Ingredients

8 cloves garlic, peeled

1 cup fresh cilantro leaves

2 limes, one juiced, one sliced thin

1 tablespoon olive oil

4 whole tilapia, scaled, gutted, and deboned

1 white onion, grated

2 teaspoons ground cumin

1 teaspoon salt

¼ teaspoon pepper

1 tablespoon butter

1 white onion, diced

1 teaspoon cinnamon

1 cup short grained white rice

2 cups milk

Preparation

Serves 4

1. Preheat oven to 350 degrees.
2. In a food processor or with a mortar and pestle, make a paste with the garlic, cilantro, and lime juice.
3. Oil 4 large sheets of aluminum foil.
4. Place a fish on each and stuff the cavities of each fish with paste.
5. Add grated onion and lime slices to each cavity.
6. Sprinkle each cavity with cumin and salt.
7. Wrap each fish and place them on a baking sheet.
8. Bake 20 minutes or until fish is white and flakes easily.

While fish is baking, prepare the rice.

1. In a 2 or 3 quart saucepan, sauté diced onion in butter over low heat until soft and transparent.
2. Add cinnamon and rice to pan and sauté 1 minute, stirring constantly.
3. Add milk, raise heat, and bring to a quick boil.
4. Cover, reduce heat to low, and simmer slowly for 20 minutes.
5. Serve rice topped with fish and drizzled with pan juices.

Okra

Okra is a flowering plant in the mallow family that was brought to the American south by African slaves. It is valued for its edible green seed pods that are high in phosphates, vitamin C, calcium, and potassium. When cooked a characteristic "goo" or slime appears; this mucilage contains a usable form of soluble fiber.

Koshari (Lentil, Rice, Macaroni, and Chickpea Casserole)

This popular Egyptian dish combines flavors from across the Eastern Mediterranean. It may be served at lunch or dinner and is often sold at street stalls. Economical and nutritious, the combination of grains and legumes produces a complete protein, so the result is not only tasty, but also good for you.

Ingredients

¾ cup brown lentils

¾ cup long-grained white rice

1 cup elbow macaroni

¾ cup canola oil

4 cloves garlic, minced

½ cup white wine vinegar

One 15-ounce can tomato puree

1 teaspoon salt

¼ teaspoon ground red pepper

1 teaspoon cumin

2 large white onions, sliced

One 15-ounce can chickpeas, rinsed well

Preparation

Serves 6-8

1. Rinse lentils and bring to boil in a large saucepan, with water to cover by 2 inches.
2. Simmer over medium heat 25 minutes, then drain.
3. Return lentils to saucepan; add rice and water to cover by 2 inches. Bring to a boil, reduce to a simmer, and cook 20 minutes or until rice and lentils are tender. Drain and set aside.
4. Cook macaroni according to package directions. Drain and set aside.
5. In a medium skillet or saucepan, heat ¼ cup oil to shimmering over medium heat.
6. Add garlic and cook 1 minute, stirring constantly. Add vinegar and cook 1 minute, stirring constantly.
7. Add tomato puree, salt, pepper, and cumin. Combine well and bring to a boil. Reduce to a simmer and cover.
8. Heat oven to 375 degrees.
9. In a separate skillet, heat the remaining oil over medium high until shimmering but not smoking.
10. Fry the onions until golden. Remove and drain on a paper towel.
11. Stir 1 tablespoon of the oil used for frying onions into the macaroni.
12. Butter the inside of a 2 or 3 quart casserole and layer ingredients as follows:
    - Layer of ½ of lentil rice mixture
    - Layer of ½ macaroni
    - Layer of ½ tomato sauce
    - Layer of ½ chickpeas
    - Layer of ½ fried onions
13. Repeat layering of ingredients. Bake 15-20 minutes until heated through.

Lentils
Lentils are one of the oldest cultivated foods. Archaeological remains of lentil seeds have been dated to 6000 BCE in Mesopotamia and Egypt. Presently, they grow and are consumed virtually all over the world in both arid and humid conditions. Lentils are an inexpensive source of protein, especially in Asia and India, where there are large vegetarian populations.

Fresh Fava Salad

Fava beans, or broad beans, have been featured in Egyptian cooking since the time of the pharaohs. In fact, Ful Medames, *a mild stew of dried favas, is called the "national dish of Egypt." Here the fresh bean, beautifully green, is featured in a simple, lightly dressed salad, suitable for a spring luncheon. Preparing fresh favas is well worth the effort.*

Ingredients

2 pounds fresh fava (broad) bean pods

1 cup grape tomatoes, halved

3 tablespoons olive oil

1 tablespoon lemon juice

2 scallions, dark ends removed and sliced thin

2 ounces feta, crumbled

Salt and pepper to taste

Preparation

Serves 4

1. Shell beans, removing all of the white fuzzy casing.
2. Blanch beans in rapidly boiling water, 2-3 minutes. Plunge into an icy water bath to cool.
3. Drain cooled beans. Slit tough outer skin with a paring knife (or a very clean fingernail) and squeeze out the bright green beans.
4. Toss beans with remaining ingredients. Serve at room temperature.

Sweet and Sour Okra

Okra appears in recipes across the African continent. Noted for its thickening power, it is frequently found in soups and stews, not unlike the gumbos of the American South. Whole pods—fried, roasted, or sautéed—are a fresh and flavorful addition to any menu.

Ingredients

1 pound small fresh okra pods, left whole

1 tablespoon olive oil

1 tablespoon butter

2 tablespoons honey

1 lemon, zested and juiced

½ teaspoon salt

¼ teaspoon pepper

⅓ cup water

Preparation

Serves 4-6

1. Wash okra. Pat dry.
2. Heat oil and butter in large skillet until butter stops foaming.
3. Sauté okra 3-5 minutes, turning often.
4. Add honey, lemon juice, salt, pepper, and water.
5. Partially cover and simmer 10 minutes, or until okra is tender and coated with sauce.
6. Serve hot, garnished with lemon zest.

Fig and Walnut Pastry

Alcoholic beverages are frowned upon in Egypt and much of North Africa. However, fruit drinks, infused waters, teas, and coffees abound. This treat, more a cookie than a pastry, is a traditional accompaniment. Flavors of figs, walnuts, and citrus are frequently combined in the salads and baked goods of the region.

Ingredients

2 cups flour

1 cup butter

¼ teaspoon salt

¼ cup orange juice

2 tablespoons milk

1 cup walnuts, crushed very fine

½ cup finely minced fresh figs

1 teaspoon cinnamon

4 teaspoons powdered sugar, total

Preparation

Yield 18 pastries

1. Preheat oven to 375 degrees.
2. Cut butter into flour until dough resembles fine crumbs.
3. Toss ¼ cup crushed walnuts into flour mixture.
4. Slowly add 2 tablespoons orange juice and 2 tablespoons milk, tossing constantly with a fork. Combine thoroughly.
5. Turn dough onto a floured surface and knead 3 minutes.
6. To make the filling, mix remaining walnuts and orange juice with figs, cinnamon, and 2 tablespoons powdered sugar.
7. Divide dough into golf ball-sized lumps and place on lightly buttered cookie sheets. Flatten into rounds, about 4 inches in diameter.
8. Place 1 teaspoon of filling onto each round. Press dough up around the filling, leaving a small circle open at the top.
9. Bake 20-25 minutes until golden brown.
10. Cool and dust with remaining powdered sugar before serving.

Figs
Figs come in many varieties ranging from pale green to black. So valued were they by the ancients that the Greeks enacted laws to forbid exporting the best. Fig trees were brought by Spanish missionaries to California where they have thrived ever since. Fresh figs are especially delicious with savories like blue cheese, ham, or olives. They are delicious eaten right from the tree, grilled, roasted, or made into jam.

Artifact

**TARENTINE RED FIGURE
BULL'S HEAD RHYTON**

Made in Apulia, Italy
ca. 350–320 BCE

Greece

From Bronze Age archaeological evidence of cooking and serving to later depictions of banqueting and feasting on reliefs, vases, and wall paintings, we know that the consumption of food has always been central to Greek identity and culture. Some of our most vivid descriptions of food and drink come from ancient Greek writers. In the 7th century BCE, the poet Alcman identified the five best wines in Greece. Hippocrates (*ca.* 460–370 BCE), the father of Western medicine, wrote extensively about nutrition. In the mid-4th century BCE, Archestratos of Syracuse wrote what may have been the first cookbook, giving explicit directions for cooking: *take a bonita fish, rub it with oregano, wrap it in fig leaves, bury it in hot ashes until done.* In the same century, Alexander the Great insisted on an apple at every meal, and, in his travels, discovered the shallot in Phoenicia, the onion in Egypt, and haricots in India. The peacock, which Alexander also encountered in India, was deemed too beautiful to kill, thus saving that magnificent bird to be savored by the Romans.

Classical Greeks valued simple, healthy foods that fed mind as well as body. Frugality was virtuous. They ate bread of barley or wheat flour, carrots, cucumbers, cabbage, garlic, onions, lentils, peas and beans boiled or mashed with lemon and oil, fruits (figs, pomegranates, and raisins), nuts, and, of course, cheese. Tradition held that beans, peas, and lentils disposed the mind to study, that cabbage should be eaten by mothers of newborns, that garlic cured low blood pressure, that watercress eased toothache, and that parsley stimulated the imagination. Some meat was consumed—pig, lamb, and goat—but very little beef, as land in many areas was rocky and too poor for grazing. Beef was eaten by the rich, was intended for sacrifices to the gods, and was presented to victors in athletic games.

The transition in Greece from simple dishes using fresh, local ingredients to a more varied cuisine is owed in part to centuries of assimilation and exchange. For more than 1,000 years (*ca.* 400–1453 CE), Greece was part of the Byzantine Empire. During

Tarentine Red Figure Bull's Head Rhyton
With its bull's-head base, this drinking vessel cannot be put down until it has been drained of its contents. Museum object #L-64-227 (on loan from the Philadelphia Museum of Art)

those years, new ingredients were introduced from the East, such as spices and sweet meats, and, after 1453, when Constantinople fell to the Ottomans, new dishes: *moussaka* (eggplant and ground lamb spiced with cinnamon, layered and topped with béchamel sauce), *tzatziki* (yogurt with cucumber and garlic), *dolmades* (stuffed grape leaves), *keftedes* (spiced meatballs), and *hummus*, from the Arabic word for chickpeas. All these dishes, though typically Greek in our minds, derive from Turkish models. And Greece continued to incorporate new ingredients into established cuisine. Tomatoes, the foundation of many of its contemporary dishes, arrived from the New World via Italy only in the early 19th century.

The quintessential elements in Greek cooking are grain, wine, olive oil, and fresh vegetables, and the greatest of these is olive oil. In a contest to name the city of Athens, Athena won by throwing a seed that grew into an olive tree, defeating Poseidon who had struck a rock from which gushed water. In the 2nd century CE, Pausanias, a Greek traveler and writer, claims to have been shown the very tree, still growing on the Acropolis. Hercules' arrows were made of olive wood. And the olive tree appears on ancient Athenian coins, its branch a symbol of victory, peace, wisdom, and prosperity. An olive wreath was awarded to winners in the Olympic Games, a tradition brought back for the 2004 Games in Athens. The first crop of olives does not appear until a tree is about five years old, yet trees are known to live for well over 1,000 years. The fruit, the oil, and even the wood continue to be important trade goods in the Mediterranean world. It is hard to find a Greek recipe that does not list olive oil as an ingredient.

Demeter (or Ceres) is believed to have taught men to cultivate wheat. In Classical times the bread of Athens was particularly renowned—over 70 different varieties existed, using varying amounts of barley or wheat flour, oil, honey, cheese, and wine. *Tsoureki*, a special Easter bread still eaten at holiday celebrations today, is flavored with oranges, nuts, and spices.

Wine has been consumed in Greece for over 6,000 years. Heavy and sweet, it was always diluted, usually three parts wine to five parts water. Hippocrates encouraged men to seek mirth through wine, which they did enthusiastically at *symposia*, drinking parties, when men reclined on couches. After a libation to the gods, they were entertained by dancers, acrobats, and musicians; they composed and recited poetry; and they drank

Artifact

MINOAN COOKING POT
Gournia, Crete
ca. 1700–1425 BCE

Minoan Cooking Pot
This small tripod cooking pot would have been placed over a fire. Museum object #MS4143

Archaic Period Silver Coin
The ear of barley on this *stater* (a denomination in Greek currency) is probably meant to celebrate the agricultural wealth of the Greek colony of Metapontum. Museum object #29-126-21

Artifact

ARCHAIC PERIOD SILVER COIN
Metapontum, Italy
ca. 520–500 BCE

Artifact

ATTIC RED FIGURE KYLIX
BY THE FOUNDRY PAINTER

Made in Athens, Greece
ca. 480 BCE

heavily, discussing weighty matters, sometimes intellectual, sometimes not. Symposia were often depicted on classic Greek vases designed to hold wine: the *amphora* to transport and store it, the *krater* in which to mix it with water, the *psykter* to cool it, the *oinochoe* to pour it into drinking cups: the *kylix, skyphos,* or *kantharos.* Today, the best wines are often said to be from Macedonia or Crete. *Retsina,* a white or rosé wine that tastes strongly of the pine resin used for centuries to seal the bottles, was quite popular until more recent times because it complemented Greek food. Although retsina is still consumed by many Greeks today, French vines have been introduced to support local wine production and to improve quality.

Modern Greeks eat sparingly at breakfast. A cup of very dense coffee, considered highly nutritious, a slice of bread, or yogurt with honey, might be followed later in the morning by a *spanakopita* (spinach pie), a *tyropita* (cheese pie), or another popular street food such as a *gyro* or *souvlakia.* Lunch is from two or three o'clock to four or five o'clock in the late afternoon. Along with local vegetables—beans, zucchini, artichokes, leafy greens cooked in olive oil with onions, garlic, fennel, tomatoes, and lemon—fish is popular on the coast or on the islands as Greeks insist that it be fresh.

Though Odysseus (or Ulysses) said disparagingly that fish should be eaten only if one is starving, early sources list an extraordinary variety: along with the familiar turbot, mullet, trout, whiting, sea bass, and perch are sea eel, dragon weaver, loach, gudgeon, sea hedgehog, and a "frightful" fish, described as having numerous legs that stretched far over the sides of the dish. Poultry (chicken, duck, and goose) is widely available. Lamb, goat, or pig, less often beef, might mark a special occasion. For example, at Easter, a whole lamb or kid is rubbed with oil, oregano, lemon, and rosemary and roasted on a spit for five to six hours. Dinner, occurring at nine or ten in the evening, may consist of a normal meal or perhaps *mezedes* (appetizers): a number of small dishes, such as salad with feta, deep-fried eggplant or zucchini, *kalamari* (squid), *dolmades,* or *taramosalata* with pita bread, accompanied by *ouzo,* an anise flavored liqueur.

Since Greek cuisine emphasizes plant-based foods, cheeses, fruits, nuts, grains, and vegetables, and the use of olive oil instead of butter, it is no wonder that Greek food (along with that of southern Italy) forms the basis of the popular "Mediterranean Diet," which is believed to prolong life.

Artifact

MYCENAEAN STIRRUP JAR

Mediterranean
1200–1100 BCE

Attic Red Figure Kylix by the Foundry Painter
Vessels such as this served as drinking cups at Greek banquets or symposia. The double-handled form, also carried by the man illustrated on the kylix, made it easier to pass the cup from person to person, demonstrating the social role that dining played in ancient Greek culture. Museum object #31-19-2

Mycenaean Stirrup Jar
The stirrup jar, a container for oil or wine, was a popular shape in the Bronze Age Aegean. The stylized octopus that decorates the vase reflects the importance of the sea in ancient Greece. Museum object #30-44-2

Olive Oil

Olive oil, with its many uses, was highly valued by numerous early cultures. It fueled the Maccabees' escape from Egypt. Catholics used it in baptisms, ordinations, and confirmations. The prophet Muhammad praised its medicinal qualities. It was responsible for the earliest Olympic flame. Produced as early as *ca.* 4000 BCE, possibly in Crete, olive oil may have contributed to the growth of the Minoan civilization. *Pithoi*, large clay jars used for the storage of oil and other commodities, have been excavated from Bronze Age palaces in Crete. Ancient millstones and presses, used to extract the oil from its fruit, have also been found across the Mediterranean.

Ancient Greeks understood the restorative qualities of olive oil and used it as a cleanser and moisturizer. Olive oil was also utilized to massage the tired muscles of athletes, and it became a popular ingredient in soaps. Most significant, however, is its use in cooking. It is one of the most delicious ingredients for dressing salads and sautéing vegetables, fish, poultry, and meats. It adds richness to any dish, and the Greeks use it liberally. Greece is the third largest producer of olive oil, after Spain and Italy. Yet Greece has the highest annual consumption of any olive oil producing country, at over 26 liters per person. Fortunately, olive oil is a "heart-healthy" monounsaturated fat that helps lower cholesterol.

Olive oil is no less valued today than it was in ancient time and, in Europe, its production is regulated as carefully as that of fine wines. Like vintage wines, olive oils vary by region and year of production and are graded according to the means of production, use of chemicals, and flavor. The highest grade is extra virgin, which must be produced in a press without heat or chemicals, measure less than 1% acidity, and be judged "superior" in taste. This beautiful green oil should be treated with care. It is best stored in a cool place and consumed within a year of pressing. Use lesser grades in recipes calling for large quantities or high heat. For a bottle of fine artisanal olive oil, you may pay as much as $100.

Campanian Red Figure Plate by the Palmer-Scallop Painter
Two large fish, bream or perch, and a smaller torpedo fish decorate this plate, which has a central indentation, perhaps for dipping sauce. Fish played a significant role in the ancient Greek diet. Museum object #MS5696

Artifact

Recipes

Avgolemono
Lemon Rice Soup

Taramosolata
Caviar Dip

Artichokes Stuffed
with Olives, Anchovies,
and Pine Nuts

Horiatiki Salata
Greek Salad
(pictured)

Grilled Branzini

Arni Sto Fourno
Roast Lamb

Moussaka
Eggplant and Lamb
Casserole

Braised Carrots
with Olives

Honey, Walnut,
and Orange Cake

Yiayia's Galaktoboureko
Custard Filled Baklava

Avgolemono (Lemon Rice Soup)

This delicious combination of classic Greek flavors is quick and easy to prepare. Served warm, it becomes comfort food for a chilly fall luncheon. Served chilled, it is a lovely start to a summer supper.

Ingredients

8 cups hearty chicken stock

½ cup Arborio rice

4 eggs, beaten

2 lemons, juiced

¼ cup chopped parsley

½ teaspoon salt

½ teaspoon black pepper

Preparation

Serves 6

1. Bring stock to a boil. Add rice. Reduce to medium-low and simmer, partially covered, until rice is very tender, about 25-30 minutes.
2. Remove from heat. Slowly whisk one cup of soup into eggs, stirring constantly.
3. Slowly pour egg mixture back into soup, stirring constantly. Raise heat and stir until thickened slightly.
4. Remove from heat and stir in lemon, parsley, salt, and pepper. Serve warm or chilled.

Taramosolata (Caviar Dip)

This recipe has been prepared for centuries and makes a classic Greek starter with a glass of chilled Ouzo and an array of fresh crisp vegetables for dipping. Tamara is available in specialty shops or online and is a critical component of the dish. Substituting other roe (caviar), such as salmon or lumpfish, is needlessly expensive and moves the dish away from its Greek roots.

Ingredients

3 slices white bread, crusts removed

¼ cup water

5 ounces Tamara (carp roe)

1 tablespoon onion, minced

1 egg yolk

1 cup olive oil

3 tablespoons lemon juice

2 tablespoons minced parsley

Preparation

Yield 1 ½ cups

1. Soak bread in water until soft. Squeeze out moisture and crumble into food processor.
2. Add Tamara, onion, and egg yolk. Combine well at medium speed.
3. Slowly drizzle in olive oil, at medium speed, until consistency of mayonnaise.
4. Add lemon and parsley. Mix thoroughly.
5. Chill thoroughly before serving.

Artichokes Stuffed with Olives, Anchovies, and Pine Nuts

Artichokes are enjoyed throughout the Mediterranean. Their preparation is always a labor of love but the results never fail to please. This dish makes a substantial first course, a perfect side for grilled meats, or a great lunch all on its own.

Ingredients

6 large artichokes

2 lemons, juiced

⅓ cup capers

¾ cup olives, pitted and chopped fine

1 cup fresh breadcrumbs

2 tablespoons basil, minced

½ cup Italian parsley, minced

6 anchovy filets

½ cup pine nuts, chopped fine

1 cup olive oil

2 lemons, cut into wedges

Preparation

Serves 6

1. Place ½ of lemon juice in large bowl of ice water.
2. Remove tough outer leaves from artichokes, cut off stems, and snip off points of leaves. Place prepared artichokes in ice bath to prevent discoloration.
3. When all artichokes have been prepared as above, place them in a saucepan with water to cover. Add remaining lemon juice. Bring to boil and simmer 20 minutes.
4. Meanwhile, combine capers, olives, breadcrumbs, basil, parsley, anchovies, pine nuts, and ½ cup olive oil to form a stuffing.
5. Preheat oven to 350 degrees.
6. Drain artichokes. Scoop out the hairy choke and discard.
7. Place in a single layer in a baking dish. Stuff and drizzle with remaining oil.
8. Bake 30-40 minutes until nicely browned.
9. Serve with lemon wedges.

Lemons

The lemon is used throughout the world in cooking, in traditional medicines, and as a cleaning agent. Thought to originate in Asia, over a dozen varieties are now cultivated. The juice, the rind, and the zest of the lemon are common ingredients in cooking, in both food and beverages. On the California coast, lemon trees bloom and produce fruit year round. Unlike other citrus trees, the lemon tree has sharp thorns.

Horiatiki Salata (Greek Salad)

The quality of the tomatoes is critical to the success of this salad. If you can not wait for the season's best, substitute 6 ripe plum tomatoes cut in quarters, or 26 cherry tomatoes cut in halves. Greeks typically do not use vinegar or include lettuce, but feel free to add if you wish. If adding vinegar, 2 tablespoons of red wine vinegar will do.

Ingredients

3 large fresh summer tomatoes, cut in chunks

1 small green bell pepper, seeded and sliced thin

1 small cucumber, peeled, seeded, and sliced thin

¼ cup red onion, sliced thin

½ cup Greek olives, pitted

1 tablespoon chopped fresh oregano, or 1 teaspoon dried

½ teaspoon salt

¼ cup extra virgin olive oil

¼ pound crumbled feta cheese

Fresh ground pepper

Preparation

Serves 6

1. Combine tomatoes, pepper, cucumber, onion, olives, oregano, salt, and olive oil. Toss well.
2. Add feta, tossing lightly.
3. Serve with a generous grind of black pepper.

Grilled Branzini

This could not be simpler or more characteristic of Greek cuisine. Your fishmonger will do all the work. All you need is a grill and 15 minutes. This preparation works as well on a stovetop grill pan as over an open flame. Bluefish make an excellent substitution.

Ingredients

4 whole Branzini, about 1 pound each, gutted, scaled, and boned. Head removed, tail and fillets intact.

Salt and pepper

½ cup olive oil

¼ cup lemon juice

2 tablespoons chopped parsley

2 tablespoons chopped oregano

Lemon wedges for garnish

Preparation

Serves 4

1. Heat grill to medium high.
2. Rinse and dry fish. Season with salt and pepper. Coat each fish lightly with 1 teaspoon olive oil.
3. Whisk remaining oil with lemon juice, parsley, and oregano. Set sauce aside.
4. Place fillets on grill skin side down, tent lightly with foil and grill about 5 minutes per side.
5. Serve whole, drizzled with sauce.

Arni Sto Fourno (Roast Lamb)

There are countless recipes for roast lamb. This one is special. It infuses the meat with the essence of root vegetables, aromatic herbs, and the subtle piney flavor of Retsina. The preparation is straightforward. The result is succulent and delicious.

Ingredients

One 6-to 7-pound bone-in leg of lamb

1 tablespoon salt

1 tablespoon black pepper

1 head garlic, cloves separated and peeled

1 large onion, quartered

1 large carrot, quartered

1 large fennel bulb, quartered

4 sprigs each of rosemary, oregano, sage, and thyme

½ cup Retsina wine

¼ cup lemon juice

Salt and pepper to taste

Preparation

Serves 8

1. Preheat oven to 325 degrees.
2. Rub lamb with salt and pepper. Make ½ inch slits in top and side of roast. Insert ½ of garlic cloves into slits.
3. Place lamb in roasting pan and surround with remaining garlic and the onion, carrots, fennel, and herbs.
4. Add wine and lemon juice to pan.
5. Cover with aluminum foil and bake 1½ hours.
6. Remove foil. Raise temperature to 450 degrees and roast 20 minutes to brown meat.
7. Remove roast to platter and rest 20 minutes before carving.
8. Meanwhile, remove herb sprigs and discard. Using a slotted spoon, transfer the roasted vegetables to a food processor and purée.
9. Pour off most of the fat from the roasting pan, retaining the juices that remain. If necessary, deglaze with additional Retsina. Return the pureed vegetables to the pan and heat the gravy to simmering. Adjust seasonings and serve warm over sliced lamb.

Rosemary
Rosemary is a woody-stemmed, perennial herb with fragrant, evergreen needle-like leaves and is native to the Mediterranean region. Sprigs were placed in the hands of the deceased or strewn in open graves. Thought of in antiquity as a tonic or antiseptic, it was first used to flavor lamb by the Byzantines. It is a member of the mint family and drought resistant, making it easy to grow in a home garden as either an herb or an ornamental plant.

Moussaka (Eggplant and Lamb Casserole)

Perhaps one of the most recognizable Greek recipes, this casserole is a great party dish. Served with a fresh Greek salad and some crusty bread, your meal is complete. You can make the dish ahead and refrigerate overnight. Be sure to bring fully to room temperature before baking.

Ingredients

3 medium eggplants, ends removed and sliced lengthwise, ½ inch thick

3 tablespoons olive oil

½ teaspoon salt

2 cloves garlic, minced

1 large onion, diced

1½ pounds ground lamb

1 teaspoon cinnamon

1 teaspoon allspice

3 tablespoons tomato paste

1 cup dry red wine

1 tablespoon chopped mint

1 teaspoon salt

½ teaspoon pepper

3 tablespoons butter

3 tablespoons flour

1½ cups whole milk at room temperature

Pinch nutmeg

1½ cups crumbled feta cheese

2 eggs, beaten

½ cup grated parmesan cheese

Fresh ground pepper

Preparation

Serves 8-10

1. Preheat oven to 450 degrees.
2. Brush eggplant slices on both sides with oil, reserving 1 tablespoon, and place on large baking sheets. Sprinkle with salt.
3. Bake eggplant 20 minutes or until softened and golden. Remove from oven and set aside. Reduce oven temperature to 375 degrees.
4. Meanwhile, heat remaining oil in a large sauté pan and cook onion until lightly browned. Add garlic and cook 1 minute.
5. Add lamb, cinnamon, and allspice. Cook 8-10 minutes, stirring constantly over medium heat.
6. Add tomato paste, wine, mint, salt, and pepper. Simmer over low, stirring until most of the liquid is absorbed.
7. Melt butter in sauce pan over low heat. Whisk in flour and cook 1 minute, stirring constantly.
8. Slowly whisk in milk, stirring constantly. Raise heat and stir until thickened.
9. Stir in feta and nutmeg. Cool slightly.
10. Slowly whisk beaten eggs into cheese sauce, stirring 1 minute.
11. Lightly oil a 13x9" baking pan. Place half the eggplant in the baking pan. Cover with the meat mixture. Place the remaining eggplant on the meat mixture. Spread the cheese sauce over the top and sprinkle with parmesan cheese.
12. Bake 45-55 minutes at 375 degrees until bubbling and golden. Rest for 30 minutes before serving.

Eggplant
Eggplants were originally domesticated in India from the wild nightshade species and are said to have been brought to Europe by the Arabs. Cultivars vary in shape and size from long, skinny white to oval, deep purple to small, grape-sized green. The raw fruit can have a somewhat bitter taste, but when salted and pressed before cooking, it becomes tender and develops a rich, complex flavor.

Braised Carrots with Olives

This lovely preparation highlights the natural sweetness of fresh carrots. They play beautifully against the fruity brine of Kalamata olives. Dark meaty Kalamatas, named for their place of origin in the southern Peloponnese, are one of the most versatile varieties of Greek olives.

Ingredients

1 pound young carrots, peeled and sliced ½ inch thick on the diagonal

1 tablespoon honey

1 tablespoon butter

⅔ cup chicken or vegetable broth

½ cup Kalamata olives, pitted and halved

1 tablespoon fresh dill, chopped fine

Fresh ground pepper to taste

Preparation   Serves 4

1. Combine carrots, honey, butter, and broth in a medium saucepan.
2. Bring to a boil, reduce to a simmer, and partially cover.
3. Simmer over medium heat until carrots are tender and most of the liquid has evaporated, about 20 minutes.
4. Uncover and add olives. Cook about 1-2 minutes, just until olives are heated through.
5. Transfer to a serving dish and garnish with dill and fresh ground pepper.

Honey, Walnut, and Orange Cake

Greeks like their desserts and many include a drizzle of a sweet citrus syrup. This classic combination of flavors harkens to the Baklava so many recognize, but is much easier to prepare. Pared with mint tea, this would be a lovely conclusion to any meal.

Ingredients

½ cup butter at room temperature

1 cup sugar

2 eggs

1 cup flour

1 cup finely chopped walnuts

1 ½ teaspoons baking powder

½ teaspoon salt

¼ cup light cream

1 orange, zested and juiced

¼ cup honey

Powdered sugar for dusting

Preparation   Serves 6-8

1. Preheat oven to 350 degrees.
2. Grease and flour 9" cake pan.
3. Cream butter and sugar until very light yellow.
4. Add eggs, one at a time, beating 1 minute after each.
5. In a separate bowl, combine flour, walnuts, baking powder, and salt.
6. Add flour mixture alternately with cream.
7. Stir zest into batter and pour into prepared pan.
8. Bake 35-40 minutes or until toothpick inserted in middle comes out clean.
9. Cool in pan 15 minutes. Invert onto rack over wax paper.
10. Mix honey and orange juice. Pour over warm cake.
11. When cake is thoroughly cool, transfer to a platter and dust with powdered sugar.

Yiayia's Galaktoboureko (Custard Filled Baklava)

If you had a Greek grandmother (Yiayia) she might have shared this family recipe with you. Here a classic semolina-based vanilla custard is encased by crispy phyllo dough and bathed in a lemon honey syrup. This labor of love yields heavenly results.

Ingredients

2 cups whole milk

⅓ cup fine semolina flour

¼ cup sugar

1 tablespoon butter

1 teaspoon vanilla

2 eggs, beaten

⅓ package phyllo dough

1 stick unsalted butter, melted

⅔ cups honey

⅓ cup water

1 teaspoon lemon juice

½ stick cinnamon

1 teaspoon ground cinnamon

Preparation

Serves 12-16

1. Combine milk, semolina, sugar, and butter in a medium saucepan. Cook over medium heat, stirring constantly, until thick and creamy. Stir in vanilla.

2. Remove from heat and cool 10 minutes.

3. Slowly whisk beaten eggs into mixture, then whisk vigorously 1 minute. Cover and cool to room temperature.

4. Preheat oven to 350 degrees.

5. Melt the stick of butter and cool to room temperature.

6. Butter an 8x8" baking pan and line with ½ phyllo dough, brushing each sheet with melted butter.

7. Carefully spread custard over phyllo. Be sure to spread to edges and corners.

8. Cover the custard with remaining phyllo, brushing each sheet with melted butter.

9. Score the top few sheets of phyllo on the diagonal with a sharp knife, about every 3 inches, forming diamond shaped sections for serving.

10. Bake 40-45 minutes until top is browned and filling is bubbling.

11. While the *Galaktoboureko* is baking, combine honey, water, lemon juice and ½ stick cinnamon in a medium saucepan. Bring to a boil, reduce to a simmer, and cook 10 minutes to form a syrup. Remove cinnamon stick and cool.

12. When *Galaktoboureko* has been removed from the oven, pour syrup over the top. Sprinkle with ground cinnamon and cool to room temperature before serving.

Honey
Honey is mentioned in both the Old and New Testaments and plays a part in the religious festivals of Hindus, Buddhists, and Muslims. The Egyptians used it in the embalming process. Pythagoras would eat nothing else with his bread and so lived into his 90s. Appreciated in civilizations from China to Mesoamerica as excellent for the health, it is an ingredient in bread, in beer, and in any number of medicines.

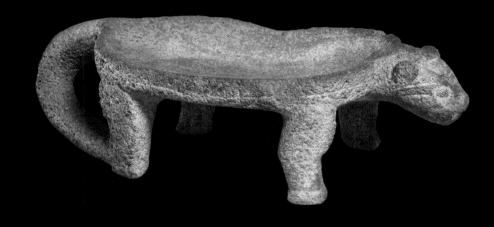

Artifact

METATE GRINDING STONE

Costa Rica

900–1200 CE

Mesoamerica

Mesoamerica—a cultural area that includes Mexico, Guatemala, Belize, El Salvador, Honduras, Nicaragua, and Costa Rica—is known for the many magnificent pre-Columbian sites that flourished here before the arrival of conquistadores in the 16th century. The first inhabitants in this part of the Americas were hunter/gatherers. But by *ca.* 4000 BCE, maize was cultivated along with beans, tomatoes, peppers, and squash by people living in settled communities. Villages grew into towns, some of which became great ceremonial centers with monumental architecture and complex socio-political systems. Mesoamerica was one of only five regions in the world where writing developed independently. Calendrical and numerical systems were created here as well. Mesoamerica has a varied ecology and includes tropical coastal lowlands along the oceans as well as cool, dry highlands in the interior and in the north. Land, sea, and river trade networks linked various communities and allowed for the transfer of raw materials and finished goods such as cotton, jade, obsidian, cacao, vanilla, salt, jaguar skins, and dried fish.

Ancient myths connected food with everyday life and religious beliefs. Mesoamerican cultures, including the Olmec, the Maya, and the Aztec, all worshipped maize gods, although the form could be female or male. The Maya Maize God was associated with both fertility and the cycle of nature. As a man, he is frequently depicted in his youth as beautiful and fertile; later, he is decapitated and then replanted, eventually springing back to life. This cycle echoes the agricultural process in which food, the source of life, must be destroyed to live again. This myth is externalized through religious rituals, which endorse periods of fasting and feasting. Maize was also an important part of the Mesoamerican diet, providing necessary calories. It could be easily ground and processed, and became an indispensable commodity and dietary staple throughout the Americas.

Maize is still the essential ingredient in the Mesoamerican diet. However, to soften the

Artifact

CERAMIC PLATE
Sitio Conte, Panama
150 BCE–300 CE

Metate Grinding Stone
Small metates such as this one were often used to grind seeds and beans. The animal depicted here may be a jaguar or other feline native to the region. Museum object #39-29-3

Ceramic Plate
This ceramic plate, characteristic of the Coclé culture located to the south of Mesoamerica, includes a red and sepia painted interior. Designs, painted on a white base, feature two red bands enclosing a scroll-like motif. Museum object #40-16-810

raw seeds and to increase their nutritional value, the kernels must be put through a process called *nixtamalization*. The corn is boiled in lime water and ash, allowing the absorption of niacin and the amino acids, lysine and tryptophan. The resulting product is then ground and made into a dough called *masa*, which is pressed into flat cakes that take many forms. *Tortillas, quesadillas, tacos, tostadas,* and *enchiladas* are just a few of the ways masa is used as a wrapper, a scoop, or even a plate. These breads may be grilled, fried, baked, or boiled, and served flat or folded to accompany other food. Masa, as well as the toppings and stuffings used with it, has regional variation. This is the magic of Mesoamerican cookery. Vegetables, meats, fish, and spices are combined in infinite variety. In some regions, filled *tamales* are wrapped in corn husks, banana leaves, or avocado leaves, and boiled, roasted, or buried in fire pits.

Artifact

CYLINDER VESSEL
Chama, Guatemala
Classic Maya
700–900 CE

Another important food was *cacao* (pronounced ka-COW). Cacao seeds come from pods, the fruit of an evergreen tree, the *Theobroma cacao*. The seeds, sometimes called beans, are now used in making chocolate. Cacao seeds are quite bitter and may not have initially been thought of as edible. In ancient times, cacao was not transformed into chocolate as we know it today. The beans were fermented, roasted, ground into a paste, mixed with water, chilies, other spices, and made into a beverage for elites, who sometimes mixed it with hallucinogenics such as mushrooms or morning glory seeds. The centrality of cacao is reflected in Maya iconography. Scenes depicting kings waiting to be served or drinking cacao decorate Maya pottery. The Penn Museum has several pots in which the residue of a chocolate drink was discovered. This custom of drinking chocolate was later introduced to Europe's upper classes by the conquistadores.

Prior to the arrival of the Spanish and the Portuguese, ducks, hairless dogs, and turkeys had been domesticated for food, wild rabbits and birds were hunted, and insects were collected. Iguanas, tortoises, armadillos, and lizards were also enjoyed as food, and, along the coasts, fish and shellfish were eaten. Ordinary people ate corn products, beans, chili peppers (almost a hundred varieties), squashes, tomatoes, tomatillos, jicamas, avocados, pumpkins, and peanuts, combined in stews and sauces (*moles*) that were highly spiced and served alongside, stuffed into, or on top of corn-based flatbreads. Fruits, such as pineapples, guavas, papayas, coconuts, bananas, and mangos were prized.

Cylinder Vessel
This large painted polychrome drinking cup features depictions of the Rabbit God, who was considered a scribe in Maya tradition. This cylinder would have been used for ritual beverages such as cacao. Museum object #NA11185

Guatemalan Monkey Vase
Alabaster effigy vases, such as this monkey vase, were used for drinking chocolate beverages. The monkey's head and arms are carved in relief. The legs and tail (not seen in this image) are also depicted. Museum object #12681

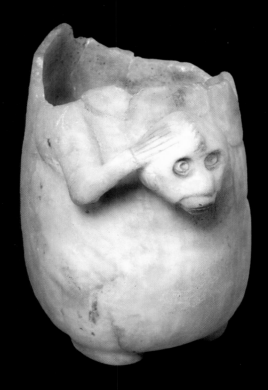

Artifact

GUATEMALAN MONKEY VASE

Escuintla, Guatemala

1000–1500 CE

Artifact

**CHOCOTEGAN MANO
AND METATE**

Guatemala or Nicaragua

300–800 CE

In the past and still in remote areas, a woman prepares food sitting on the ground or on a low stool or chair. Her main cooking implements are a stone *metate* (a mortar) and a *mano* (a hand roller) for grinding corn, chilies, or cacao; a grater for shredding yucca, plantains, cassava, or coconut; a *comal* (a stone or iron griddle) for cooking tortillas; and a *cazuela* or casserole for moles and stews. She cooks with pork fat or palm oil, although olive oil is increasingly popular. She may be superstitious. She never stirs with a knife, a symbol of strife. She believes that a fierce gaze can ruin a dish. She is careful not to spill corn lest she anger the corn deity.

The Mesoamerican cook chooses her spices carefully for maximum flavor and color. A recipe may list four or five different ones. Some arrived from the Old World: anise, saffron, cinnamon, bay, and cloves, but many were native plants: allspice, cilantro, *epazote, achiote, hierba santa*, and vanilla. Chili peppers are ubiquitous. Rare is a recipe that does not call for *serranos, poblanos, quajillos, anchos,* or *chipotles.* Each country and each region within a country has its favorite chilies, and proportions vary when blended with meat, fish, vegetables, or beans. Bitter oranges and limes are squeezed over grilled or fried meat or fish for extra zing.

Some of the best Mesoamerican cooking developed under the Spanish occupation. Impressed by the sophistication of the cultures they found in the New World, the Spaniards who settled in central Mexico and other areas intermarried, which resulted in an immediate blending of foods and foodways. While the Spanish introduced cattle, sheep, pigs, and chickens, along with rice, wheat, onions, garlic, citrus fruits, and sugar cane, the locals offered corn products, tomatoes, chili peppers, avocados, cacao, vanilla, and innumerable spices.

Today, although European-style food might be consumed, there is increased interest in traditional Mesoamerican family recipes and regional differences. More fish and shellfish are eaten in lands to the south. *Ceviche* (raw fish marinated in lime juice) is popular. Grated yucca or plaintain sometimes replaces corn as a staple starch. Exotic fruits such as golden plums, custard apples, and tamarind grow in the humid climate. And coconut milk sometimes replaces cow's milk in sweet and savory dishes.

Artifact

EX VOTOS or VOTIVE OFFERING
Mexico
1900

Chocotegan Mano and Metate
Most likely made of basalt, this large, finely carved mano and metate set were used to grind grain and seeds. Notice the ornate carved head on the metate. Museum object #NA11873B and NA11872

Ex Votos or Votive Offering
An oil painting, used as a votive offering, depicts a man herding a group of pigs, set against a scenic landscape. Museum object #86-36-66

Maize

Maize is a large grain plant domesticated in Mesoamerica perhaps as early as 8000 BCE. By 2500 BCE it was propagated by the Maya, whose creation myth tells of man's formation from a stalk of maize. Easy to grow and yielding an abundant high calorie crop, it was the basic food of the Maya as well as of the Inca, Aztec, and the Native peoples of North America. Columbus brought maize to Europe where the use of its kernels, or "corns," became ingredients in gruels like polenta.

Across Mesoamerica virtually every dish uses maize in some form. Tortillas, tamales, tacos, quesadillas, enchiladas, and tostadas all begin with maize. Sauces, like the moles of Mexico and Central America, are thickened with cornstarch. Corn oil is the preferred cooking oil. Grits and cornbread are standard fare in much of the United States, especially in the south. In America, we all love popcorn and many of us grew up on cornflakes. Fine bourbon whiskey results from the careful fermentation and aging of corn.

Corn on the cob is also an American favorite. Who doesn't look forward to summer's fresh-off-the-stalk ear of corn, covered with melted butter? We are so particular about our corn on the cob that distinct regional preferences have emerged. New Englanders treasure the bi-colored variety—called "butter and sugar"—with plump yellow and white kernels. Folks in the mid-Atlantic region swear by their crisp sweet white corn, often referred to as "shoe-peg." Mid-westerners love the juicy yellow kernels of the variety that proliferates across the plains.

Today maize is the largest crop, by weight, produced worldwide, at about 332 million metric tons. The U.S. produces 40% of the world crop. In addition to its use as a foodstuff, maize is also used for fodder and in the production of sweeteners and fuel. About 40% of the yearly production is converted to ethanol, which is projected to increase as we move toward sustainable fuels.

Matlatzinga Tripod Bowl
This tripod bowl, decorated in red on buff, is made from clay and has hollow, rattling feet. Striations on the interior suggest that it was used to grate chilies. Museum object #31-41-29

Recipes

Chilled Corn and
Avocado Soup

Jicama and
Watermelon Salad

Guacamole with Jicama
(pictured)

Turkey in Mole Sauce

Chicken with Tomatillo
and Pepita Sauce

Red Snapper and
Scallop Ceviche

Drunken Beans

Aquacate Relleno
Avocado Stuffed
with Shrimp

Roasted Green Chilies
with Cream

Fresh Limas with
Lime Butter

Hot Chocolate,
Mexican Style

Chilled Corn and Avocado Soup

This cool and creamy soup is a perfect combination of flavors that are both subtle and sharp. Topped with cilantro cream, it is a beautiful first course or luncheon centerpiece.

Ingredients

2 ears fresh corn, shucked

1 quart water

1 medium onion, diced

2 cloves garlic, minced

1 teaspoon salt

1 serrano chili, seeded and minced

1 shallot, minced

2 large, very ripe Hass avocados

¼ cup lime juice

¼ cup sour cream or crema

½ cup cilantro, finely chopped

¼ cup olive oil

Preparation

Serves 4-6

1. Remove kernels from cobs. Cut cobs into quarters.
2. Bring corn kernels, cobs, water, onion, garlic, and salt to a boil in a large saucepan.
3. Reduce to a simmer and cook uncovered, until reduced to about 3 cups. Remove from heat. Discard cobs and cool.
4. Add chili and shallots to broth and purée using an immersion blender.
5. Peel, pit, and dice avocado. Add to soup with lime juice and ¼ cup cilantro. Purée.
6. Transfer soup to bowl, cover, and chill.
7. Combine sour cream, remaining cilantro, and olive oil.
8. Serve chilled soup with a dollop of cilantro cream.

Jicama and Watermelon Salad

This salad is beautiful, and it could not be easier to prepare. The flavors are fresh and perfectly balanced. And with very few calories, it is sure to become one of your go-to summer recipes.

Ingredients

1 large jicama, peeled

2 yellow bell peppers, seeded

½ seedless watermelon

⅛ cup olive oil

1 lime, zested and juiced

1 tablespoon chopped fresh oregano

½ teaspoon salt

1 pinch dry red pepper flakes

Preparation

Serves 6

1. Cut jicama and peppers into julienne strips. Use a melon baller to scoop watermelon into little round balls.
2. Toss jicama, peppers, and watermelon in large bowl.
3. In a seperate bowl, whisk olive oil, lime juice, lime zest, oregano, salt, and pepper flakes.
4. Pour dressing over jicama mixture, toss, cover, and chill 30 minutes before serving.

Guacamole with Jicama

This chunky flavor-packed guacamole is great with crisp tortilla chips. Or use it as a salsa with grilled chicken. The jicama, native to Central America, and now widely available, adds a crunchy apple-like flavor.

Ingredients

1 large tomato

3 jalapeño peppers

2 large avocados

2 tablespoons fresh lime juice

½ jicama, peeled and diced

3 scallions, sliced thin

1 garlic clove, minced

½ cup cilantro leaves, chopped fine

3 tablespoons olive oil

½ teaspoon salt

¼ teaspoon pepper

Preparation

Serves 6

1. Bring water to a rolling boil in a medium-sized saucepan. Cut a shallow X in the bottom of the tomato. Place tomato into boiling water and remove as soon as skins starts to split, about 25 seconds. Immediately run under cold water to stop the cooking process. Peel off the skin, and cut into quarters. Remove seeds and chop into small pieces. Set aside.

2. When handling jalapeño peppers, always wear plastic gloves as the oils in thier flesh can irritate the skin. Using a paring kife, cut the peppers in half lengthwise and remove the veins and the seeds. Chop the peppers into small ⅛ inch bits. Set aside.

3. Using a sharp knife, cut the avocados lengthwise around the circumference to the depth of the seed. Twist avocados to separate into halves. Remove the pits with a spoon.

4. Scoop the avocado flesh away from the skin into a medium-sized bowl. Add fresh lime juice. Using a fork, mash into a chunky mixture.

5. Add the tomatoes, jalapeño peppers, and the remaining ingredients. Mix well.

6. Cover the bowl with plastic wrap and chill for 1 hour prior to serving.

Tomatoes
Members of the nightshade species along with eggplant and tobacco, tomatoes originated in Mexico, then spread throughout the world after the Spanish conquest of the Americas. Currently, there are about 7,500 tomato varieties, including heirloom tomatoes which have become increasingly popular for their excellent flavor among home gardeners and organic producers.

Turkey in Mole Sauce

Turkey is native to the Americas and mole, in its many variations, is revered across Mesoamerica, especially in Mexico. This spicy combination is a great party dish. Do not be daunted by the list of ingredients; the preparation is relatively straightforward. Put it together in the morning and pop it in the oven when guests arrive. Serve with rice, beans, and a crisp green salad.

Ingredients

5-6 pounds skin-on, bone-in turkey portions (legs, thighs, breasts as preferred)

1 quart turkey stock

2 bay leaves

¼ cup corn oil

2 medium onions, chopped

4 garlic cloves, chopped

2 green bell peppers, seeded and chopped

2 tablespoons ground cumin

1 teaspoon cinnamon

½ teaspoon ground anise seed

4 tablespoons toasted sesame seeds

¾ cup unsalted roasted peanuts

4 soft tortillas, torn into small pieces

2 cups chopped tomato

3 dried ancho chilies, reconstituted and chopped

1 teaspoon salt

3 ounces unsweetened chocolate, chopped

Preparation

1. Bring stock and bay leaves to boil in large pot.
2. Add turkey pieces. Return to boil. Reduce to simmer. Cover and cook 1 hour.
3. Remove turkey pieces to a platter. Reserve stock. When turkey is cool, remove skin, bones, and cartilage. Tear meat into large chunks and place in 9x13" baking dish.
4. Heat 2 tablespoons oil and sauté onion, garlic, and green pepper until very soft.
5. Transfer onion mixture to a food processor. Add 1 cup reserved stock, cumin, cinnamon, anise seed, sesame seed, peanuts, tortilla pieces, tomatoes, and ancho chilies. Purée until very smooth.
6. Preheat oven to 325 degrees.
7. Heat remaining oil in large skillet. Add puréed mixture and simmer 15 minutes, stirring constantly.
8. Stir chocolate, salt, and remaining stock into sauce. Whisk until chocolate melts.
9. Pour sauce over turkey in casserole and bake covered 1 hour. Serve.

Serves 8-10

Chili Peppers
Chili peppers are *capsicums*, in the same family as bell peppers and paprika pods. They range in flavor from rich and sweet to fiery hot. Archaeological evidence from sites in Ecuador indicates that chili peppers were domesticated thousands of years ago.

Chicken with Tomatillo and Pepita Sauce

The sauce is like a thick cream. The chicken is moist and succulent under its pale green blanket. This dish is a labor of love but the results are well worth every moment of preparation. Spend a rainy afternoon in the kitchen and serve your favorite friends this winning dish.

Ingredients

8 large boneless, skinless chicken breasts

1 head garlic, halved

1 large onion, halved

1 small bunch cilantro, tied

1 teaspoon salt

6 peppercorns

6 allspice berries

1 cup pepitas (pumpkin seeds)

2 tablespoons sesame seeds

4 whole cloves

Pinch red pepper flakes

One 28-ounce can tomatillos

6 serrano chilies, seeded and minced

1 poblano chili, seeded and minced

1 medium onion, chopped

1 tablespoon minced garlic

2 tablespoons salt

¼ cup corn oil

¼ cup chopped cilantro

Preparation

Serves 8

1. Place chicken, garlic, onion, cilantro, peppercorns, and allspice berries in a large pot. Cover with water. Bring to a boil. Reduce to simmer, cover, and cook 15 minutes over low heat.

2. Remove chicken breasts to 9x13" baking dish.

3. Continue simmering stock, covered, for 45 minutes. Cool, strain, and reserve liquid.

4. Heat a large skillet and toast pepitas, sesame seeds, cloves, and red pepper flakes for 2 minutes. Remove to small bowl and cool. Grind to fine powder in a coffee or spice grinder.

5. Purée drained tomatillos, serranos, poblanos, onion, garlic, and salt in a blender.

6. Heat oil in large saucepan. Add tomatillo purée. Simmer 5 minutes, stirring.

7. Add 3 cups reserved stock and pepita spice mixture. Simmer sauce 20 minutes.

8. Preheat oven to 350 degrees.

9. Pour sauce over chicken and bake 30-35 minutes until heated through and bubbling.

10. Sprinkle with cilantro before serving.

Tomatillos
The tomatillo fruit is surrounded by an inedible, paper-like husk. As the fruit matures, it fills the husk, splits open, and then browns by harvest time. After the husk has been removed, it can be eaten raw as the main diced ingredient in green salsa, or cooked and puréed into a sauce.

Red Snapper and Scallop Ceviche

Ceviche has been prepared in coastal regions of Mesoamerica for millennia. The almost magical ability of citrus to "cook" seafood and the simplicity of preparation makes this a dish worthy of experimentation. Try shrimp in place of scallops, grapefruit in place of blood oranges, or jalapeño instead of serrano.

Ingredients

2 pounds skinned red snapper fillets cut into ½ inch cubes

1 pound sea scallops, quartered

1 large shallot, minced

2 blood oranges, sectioned

1 serrano chili, seeded and minced

1 tablespoon olive oil

1 tablespoon salt

1 tablespoon fresh oregano, chopped

1 tablespoon fresh cilantro, chopped

1 pinch red pepper flakes

½ cup fresh lime juice

¼ cup fresh lemon juice

Preparation

Serves 6-8

1. Combine snapper, scallops, shallot, orange, chili, oil, salt, oregano, cilantro, and pepper flakes in non-reactive 9x12" baking dish.
2. Combine lemon and lime juice. Pour over seafood mixture.
3. Cover and refrigerate 1 hour or until fish is opaque. Serve.

Drunken Beans

These are baked beans, Mexican style. You will never go back to the bland New England version after you have tried these. Oregano, jalapeño, and beer add just the right undertones to the pinto beans. These are even better the second day!

Ingredients

1 pound dry pinto beans

½ pound bacon, chopped

1 large onion, chopped

2 cloves garlic, peeled and sliced

2 tablespoons fresh oregano leaves

1 jalapeño pepper, seeded and minced

1 bottle dark Mexican beer

1 quart water

2 cups chopped tomato

1 tablespoon salt

Preparation

Serves 8-10

1. Cover beans with water and soak overnight. Drain.
2. Preheat oven to 300 degrees.
3. In large Dutch oven, fry bacon, onion, and garlic until onions are browned.
4. Add oregano, jalapeño, beer, water, tomatoes, and bring to a boil. Add beans and return to a boil.
5. Cover pot and bake 2 hours, until beans are softened.
6. Add salt, stir completely, and bake uncovered 15-30 minutes until beans are soft and liquid is mostly absorbed.
7. Adjust seasoning and serve.

Aguacate Relleno (Avocado Stuffed with Shrimp)

The perfect dish for a summer luncheon, this is as pretty and simple as can be. Shrimp, avocado, and lime work beautifully together, and the cilantro adds just the right zing. Just be sure the avocados are at their peak.

Ingredients

1 pound medium-sized cooked shrimp (peeled and deveined)

½ cup red onion, diced

½ cup red bell pepper, diced

¼ cup chopped cilantro

¼ cup mayonnaise (more or less according to preferences)

2 limes, juiced

Salt/pepper to taste

4 firm ripe avocados

1 small head butter lettuce, leaves separated and washed

Preparation

Serves 8

1. Chop shrimp into bite-sized pieces.
2. Combine diced onions, red pepper, shrimp, juice of 1 lime, 2 tablespoons chopped cilantro, and mayonnaise.
3. Taste, and add salt and pepper to taste.
4. Cut avocados in half, remove seed and peel carefully.
5. Plate lettuce leaves and top with avocados.
6. Drizzle remaining lime juice over avocados.
7. Spoon shrimp mixture into avocado halves.
8. Sprinkle with remaining cilantro and serve.

Roasted Green Chilies with Cream

Poblano chilies have a distinctive rich flavor when roasted, so avoid the temptation to substitute other peppers in this recipe. This simple preparation would pair nicely with grilled pork chops.

Ingredients

2 pounds poblano chilies

3 tablespoons corn oil

1 large white onion, sliced

1 teaspoon salt

½ cup heavy cream

Preparation

Serves 4

1. Heat broiler.
2. Place chilies on rack in oven 2 inches below broiler flame. Roast, turning often, until thoroughly charred.
3. Place chilies in a paper bag. Twist closed. Cool 15 minutes.
4. Remove chilies from paper bag, rub-off charred skin, remove stem, seeds, and cut into ½ inch strips.
5. Heat oil in large skillet. Add onions and fry over medium-low heat until light brown.
6. Add chilies and salt. Cook 3 minutes, stirring.
7. Add cream, cook 2 minutes, stirring. Serve.

Fresh Limas with Lime Butter

Here is a simple preparation for one of summer's underappreciated vegetables. Lima beans are prolific throughout the Americas. Lime is a perfect complement to the starch in the beans, and butter makes everything better.

Ingredients

2 pounds young fresh lima beans in shells

2 cups vegetable broth

3 tablespoons butter, melted

1 lime, zested and juiced

1 tablespoon fresh oregano, chopped

1 teaspoon salt

Preparation

Serves 4

1. Shell beans.
2. Bring broth to a boil. Add beans. Return to boil. Reduce to simmer and cook, uncovered, until beans are soft but not mushy, about 20 minutes. Drain.
3. Melt butter in small sauce pan. Add zest, juice, and salt. Bring to a simmer.
4. Place beans in serving bowl. Stir in oregano. Pour lime butter over and toss.

Hot Chocolate, Mexican Style

Chocolate lovers beware. This is, bar none, the most exquisite hot chocolate you will ever taste. You will be imbibing at breakfast, mid-afternoon, before bed, or whenever you need a chocolate fix. This explains why cacao, from which chocolate is derived, is called the "food of the gods."

Ingredients

4 ounces dark semi-sweet chocolate

4 ounces dark unsweetened chocolate

1 quart whole milk

1 stick cinnamon

¼ cup dark brown sugar

½ teaspoon vanilla

2 egg whites, beaten

Preparation

Serves 6

1. Slowly melt chocolate in top of double boiler over simmering water.
2. In a separate saucepan, heat milk, cinnamon, and sugar to just below boiling. Stir in vanilla and remove cinnamon stick.
3. Whisk milk into chocolate.
4. Slowly whisk beaten egg whites into chocolate mixture.
5. Beat with rotary mixer until frothy. Serve.

Cacao Beans

The cacao tree originated in Central and South America. A glyph representing cacao is seen on some Olmec burial vases. A thick pod lined with sweet pulp contains the bitter seeds that, when roasted and fermented, are ground into a powder that is commonly called cocoa. From this powder, chocolate is made.

Artifact

GOLDEN APPLE PENDANT
Ur, Mesopotamia (Iraq)
2550–2450 BCE

Middle East

You are the guest of a well-to-do merchant in Izmir, Damascus, or Baghdad in the early 20th century. Hospitality is highly valued, and you are the recipient. To welcome is to compliment, and the food will be beautiful. With beverages, an array of *mezze* appears—small dishes, as varied in color, texture, and aroma as in taste. Larger dishes are finished with dustings of spices (turmeric or saffron for color) or elaborate arrangements of chopped nuts. The more complex the preparation, the greater the honor to the guest. This dining style has its roots in ancient Mesopotamia and even further east.

From earliest times, migrating peoples moved between east and west, bringing with them foods, carried on horse or camelback through the mostly arid lands of Central Asia. Domestic wheat, barley, chickpeas, beans, flax, and bitter vetch have been cultivated since *ca.* 8500 BCE. A grain such as wheat or barley was the first domesticated plant and is associated with the beginning of agriculture. Cuneiform tablets tell us that barley was also a currency for ancient Sumerians.

Our host in Damascus serves neither beef, needing rich grassland, nor pork, forbidden to observing Jews and Muslims. But sheep and goats, the first domesticated animals in this region, might be on the menu. We see rams, fat-tailed sheep, and goats on objects from the Museum's Ur collection, including the famous "Ram Caught in a Thicket," which is thought to be a wild male goat. These animals appear in sacred stories and on both ancient and modern Middle Eastern menus.

Throughout the Near and Middle East, cooking was deemed a high art, especially among the wealthy in the great empires—the Sassanids in Persia, 224–651 CE; the Abassids in Baghdad, 750–1250 CE; and the Ottoman Turks in Istanbul, 1299–1922 CE. In this long history, conflict, conquest, alliances, and migrations alternated with centuries of stability under autocratic dynasties. Both war and peace contributed to the variety and

Artifact

GOLD TUMBLER
Ur, Mesopotamia (Iraq)
2550–2450 BCE

Golden Apple Pendant
This small pendant of gold and carnelian is one of many ornaments that may have hung from necklaces of blue lapis lazuli beads. Originally thought to be pomegranates, they are now believed to be apples. Element from Museum object #B16684

Gold Tumbler
Many gold vessels were buried with Queen Puabi in ancient Ur. This tumbler was manufactured with a pleated, fluted shape and features incised decoration around the rim. Museum object #B17691

magnificence of cooking cultures. Visitors from Europe wrote of the lavish imperial banquets for which delicacies were imported from far away.

As one dynasty succeeded another, and as people travelled, the number of cooking ingredients grew dramatically: spices from India and China, coffee from Ethiopia, and salted fish, caviar, and honey from Russia. As Turkish tribes moved westward, the taste for milk products increased, and stuffed dumplings and meat broiled on skewers were introduced. An extraordinary example of the efficacy of trade, when peace follows conquest, is the Arab occupation of Spain (711–1492 CE), when the great sherries of Jerez in southern Iberia were developed from a root stock of grapes grown in Shiraz in Persia.

The West benefitted from similar exchanges. Crusaders, returning home from the East, introduced *Saracen* cooking to their families and friends. But conquest can also destroy: during the occupation of northern Azerbaijan by the Soviet Union in 1917, one-crop collective farming was imposed on the region. Thus rice was replaced by potatoes, favored by Russians. Spices were luxuries, so the spice markets died. The great festival meals of Ramadan were forbidden under a regime that opposed religion.

We can learn a lot about courtly cuisine from the careful household records kept in the Topkapi Palace in Istanbul. For almost 500 years of relative peace under the Ottomans (1453–1922), the cooking skills of chefs in both Europe and in the Middle East expanded. Ingredients from the Mediterranean like olives and oranges entered the repertory of eastern cooks, and France received the croissant from Turkey via Austria. Under Suleyman the Magnificent in the 16th century, palace kitchens, staffed by nearly 1,400, supported an elaborate hierarchy of specialists in soups, breads, meats, fish, *pilafs*, sweet pastries, fruit jams, or sherbets. That the symbol of each Janissary division was its *kasgan* or cooking cauldron suggests how highly esteemed was the art of cooking in the Ottoman court. The famous Egyptian Spice Bazaar, still one of the great sights of Istanbul, was supervised by guilds that regulated price and quality.

Though the seasoning varies, many rural recipes are essentially from the same ingredients, but called by different names. A dish of rice and lentils is *magadarra* in Egypt and *mudardara* in Lebanon. Of course, in the countryside the delicacies that appeared on the tables of the Ottoman sultans—rose or orange blossom water, marzipan, and

Artifact

WINE JAR

Hajii Firuz Tepe, Iran

ca. 5400–5000 BCE

Wine Jar
Found sunken into a floor, residue in this jar tested positive for wine and terebinth tree resin. It is the oldest known wine storage container in the world. Museum object #69-12-15

"Ram Caught in a Thicket"
A pair of these figures was recovered from Tomb PG 1237. Made of gold, silver, copper, shell, lapis lazuli, red limestone, and bitumen, one now resides at the British Museum and the other can be found in "Iraq's Acient Past" at the Penn Museum. Museum object #30-12-702

Artifact

"RAM CAUGHT IN A THICKET"
Ur, Mesopotamia (Iraq)
2550–2450 BCE

Artifact

SUMERIAN CUNEIFORM TABLET
Nippur, Mesopotamia (Iraq)
ca. 1750 BCE

sorbets—were largely unknown. In the villages, beans, lentils, and chickpeas are still cooked in combinations flavored with lemon and whatever herbs and spices are available. Many foods, such as peppers, potatoes, tomatoes, and sugar cane arrived from the New World via Spain in the 16th century.

Cooking was a social activity for women in the home. Cookbooks were rare until recently, though recipes were treasured and handed down in families. Directions were kept intentionally vague: *simmer until done, a pinch of this or that,* or *add water as needed.* Slow cooking was preferred; meat should fall off the bone and never be pink. At home meats were grilled, not roasted, as many families had no oven. Even now for major social gatherings, large dishes are taken to a communal oven, usually the baker's.

Traditionally, main dishes were served all at once, and eating practices were clearly defined. Wash your hands before and after eating, in finer houses, with orange or rose water. Invoke the name of God before and after the meal. Sit on the floor or on cushions around a low table. Turn your left side toward the table. Eat with three fingers, the thumb and the first two fingers. Help yourself to small amounts, and do not gaze at others while doing so. Stop eating only when all others have finished. Discuss pleasant subjects. Lick your fingers at the end of the meal only.

These customs are gradually being discarded, especially in urban areas. Women no longer eat after or separately from men. Restaurants are more popular as women work and can no longer give hours to chopping and stuffing. Meals are offered in courses, and it is hard to believe that conversation never touches on the controversial. Enormous differences—depending on the fertility of the soil, the prosperity of the population, and the dominance of Islamic custom—still exist among different local groups, countries, and cultures. Despite globalization, local Middle Eastern cooking is now increasingly celebrated. Authentic "peasant" food, earlier considered unsophisticated, has become fashionable.

Sumerian Cuneiform Tablet
This Early Old Babylonian Period clay tablet was discovered during the Penn Museum's 1889–1900 excavation at Nippur. It lists numerous foodstuffs, including soups, beers, breads, and vegetables. Museum object #B 3918 and B 3928

Barley

The wild ancestor of today's barley thrived in the grasslands of the Fertile Crescent for thousands of years before it was domesticated, possibly as early as 8500 BCE. A hearty grain, barley is tolerant of salinity, enhancing its ability to thrive under irrigation. Used as animal fodder and in porridge, breads, and beverages, barley rations were recorded on cuneiform tablets from 2350 BCE. Egyptians created a sign for barley. The Old Testament lists barley among the seven crops of the Promised Land. And barley soup was thought to lower fevers. Across the ancient Mediterranean, barley was a medium of trade and appeared on early Roman coins.

Today, wild barleys, although different from domesticated varieties, are still found growing along creeks and roadsides in various regions of the Middle East. Barley contains eight essential amino acids and is high in fiber, making it a healthy whole grain. Its nutty, chewy texture resembles brown rice, and it is a frequent ingredient in soups, stews, and vegetable salads. Although barley is a common addition to many dishes, it may be surprising to some to learn that nearly 50% of the world's barley production is used for beer.

As in the times of Queen Puabi and King Midas, fermented barley, or malt, is the basis for beer. Research by Dr. Patrick McGovern, at the Penn Museum's Biomolecular Archaeology Laboratory, has confirmed that pots found in the Midas Mound tumulus at Gordion, Turkey (*ca.* 740 BCE, now thought to contain the father of Midas) include residues of wine, mead, and barley beer. The burial tomb of Queen Puabi, *ca.* 2550–2450 BCE, unearthed at Ur in southern Iraq, contained a silver beer pot and the remains of a straw used for sipping. Cylinder seals from the Ur excavation depict royalty sipping beer from similar pots.

Beer was a preferred drink throughout much of the ancient world. By the Middle Ages barley and beer made their way across Europe where beer became an everyday beverage, especially in Northern Europe and the British Isles. There, barley was stored in barley houses, later known as barns. By the late 15th century, the Scots had devised an even more potent form of fermented barley: Scotch whiskey.

Great Lyre Panel
The front panel on the Great Lyre's soundbox is made of shell and bitumen. Four scenes relate to Mesopotamian burial practices, including eating, drinking, and playing music. Museum object #B17694A

Artifact

GREAT LYRE PANEL

Ur, Mesopotamia (Iraq)

2550–2450 BCE

Recipes

Hummus with Tahini

Baba Ghanouj
Eggplant Dip

Chilled Cucumber Soup
(pictured)

Whole Wheat
Pita Bread

Lamb and Date
Kabobs

Mahmudiye
Braised Chicken
with Grapes

Beet and Yogurt Salad

Albaloo Polo
Rice with Black Cherry

Saffron Rice Pilaf

Pomegranate
Apple Ice

Hummus with Tahini

Chickpeas form the base of most recipes for hummus, a familiar dip for pita bread and crudités. Common in Middle Eastern diets for at least 6,000 years, these legumes are a good source of protein. This combination of softened beans, lemon, and sesame is a classic.

Ingredients

1 pound chickpeas

2 garlic cloves, minced

¼ cup olive oil

1 lemon, juiced and zested

2 tablespoons ground coriander

2 tablespoons ground cumin

3 tablespoons tahini paste

1 teaspoon salt

½ teaspoon white pepper

¼ cup pine nuts, toasted

Extra virgin olive oil for finishing

Preparation

Serves 6-8 as an appetizer

1. Cook chickpeas according to package direction until tender. Drain, reserving cooking liquid.
2. Purée chickpeas, garlic, lemon juice, coriander, cumin, tahini, salt, and pepper in a food processor until very smooth.
2. Add reserved liquid, 1 tablespoon at a time, if mixture is too thick.
3. Transfer to a serving bowl and garnish with lemon zest and pine nuts. Drizzle generously with olive oil.

Chickpeas
Chickpeas or garbanzos are a type of pulse (a crop harvested solely for the dry seed), with one seedpod containing two or three peas. They are one of the earliest cultivated legumes. Remains have been found in the ancient Near East and in Europe, where they were a staple of local cuisines and were also thought to have medicinal benefit. Ground chickpeas were used as a coffee substitute during World War I in Europe.

Baba Ghanouj (Eggplant Dip)

Eggplant, native to India, made its way to the Mediterranean region as a result of trade during the Middle Ages. They now appear in a variety of preparations. Serve this traditional savory dish, sometimes called "poor man's caviar" with fresh pita bread.

Ingredients

Preparation

Serves 4-6 as an appetizer

1 large or 2 small eggplant

2 cloves garlic, minced

2 tablespoons lemon juice

¼ cup olive oil

½ cup parsley, roughly chopped

¼ cup mint, roughly chopped

1 pinch red pepper flakes

1 teaspoon salt

¼ cup pomegranate seeds (or pine nuts)

1. Heat oven to broiling.
2. Halve eggplant(s) and place on an oiled sheet, skin side up. Broil until skin is black and cracked.
3. Remove from oven and cool. Peel skin away. Place pulp in colander to drain, 10-15 minutes.
4. Place eggplant, garlic, lemon juice, olive oil, parsley, mint, pepper flakes, and salt in a food processor. Purée.
5. Transfer eggplant purée to a bowl. Stir in pomegranate seeds (or pine nuts). Cover and chill.

Chilled Cucumber Soup

Cucumbers, yogurt, and dill are all plentiful in the Middle East. No wonder they appear together in numerous recipes for soups, sauces, and salads. This cooling and lovely combination makes a delicious quick start to a summer dinner.

Ingredients

Preparation

Serves 4-6

½ cup raisins

2 cups plain whole fat yogurt

2 large cucumbers, diced

1 small onion, diced

1 clove garlic, crushed

1 ½ teaspoons salt

¼ teaspoon white pepper

½ cup whole milk

½ cup sour cream

1 tablespoon olive oil

1 tablespoon lemon juice

2 tablespoons minced fresh dill

1. Place raisins in a small bowl and cover with boiling water. Cover and steep for one half hour. Drain and pat dry. Set aside.
2. Purée remaining ingredients in a food processor until smooth. Transfer to a bowl and cover with plastic wrap. Chill until ready to serve.
2. To serve, ladle soup into individual bowls and top with raisins.

Whole Wheat Pita Bread

What can be more satisfying than the aroma of your own bread wafting through the kitchen? Even though good pita bread, a staple at Middle Eastern tables, is readily available, nothing surpasses home-baked freshness. The ingredients and preparation are straightforward. All you need is a little time.

Ingredients

Preparation

Yield 8, six inch pitas

1 package yeast

1 teaspoon honey

1¼ cups warm water

1 cup whole wheat flour

2 cups bread flour

1 tablespoon salt

¼ cup olive oil

Cornmeal

1. Dissolve yeast in honey and ½ cup water. Proof 15 minutes until foamy.
2. In a separate bowl, combine flours and salt.
3. Stir oil into yeast mixture.
4. Add flour mixture alternately with remaining water, kneading well after each addition until sticky dough forms.
5. Lightly flour a board. Turn out dough and knead 10 minutes until smooth and elastic, adding more flour if necessary. Cover and let rise until double in bulk.
6. Lightly oil a large bowl. Place dough in bowl and turn to coat surface. Cover with plastic wrap and let rise until double in size, about 2 hours.
7. Punch dough down and transfer to lightly floured board. Knead 1-2 minutes to remove any air bubbles.
8. Divide into 8 pieces. Roll each into a ball. Place dough balls on baking sheet, cover and let rest 30 minutes.
9. Flour a surface and roll balls into 6 inch rounds.
10. Dust 2 cookie sheets with corn meal and place 4 pitas on each. Cover and let rise 30 minutes.
11. Place oven rack on lowest position. Remove other racks.
12. Preheat oven to 500 degrees.
13. Using a wide flat metal spatula, transfer 4 pitas, one at a time, directly onto oven rack. Bake 2 minutes or until lightly browned. Turn with long handled tongs. Bake 1 minute more. Remove to cooling rack.
14. Repeat with remaining pitas. Serve warm.

Pomegranates

Persephone broke her fast by eating the seeds of the pomegranate and so was condemned to spend six months each year in the Underworld. Pomegranates, originating in the East, are thought to be refreshing in hot climates. Each seed is surrounded by a water-laden pulp—the edible aril, and the seeds are embedded in a white, spongy, astringent membrane.

Lamb and Date Kabobs

Grilling is an ancient and common food preparation method, especially for meats. In the Middle East lamb is the favorite. Kabobs, meats skewered and grilled over an open fire, are classic fare. Here, the lamb is enhanced by a delicious marinade of yogurt and spices and grilled with sweet succulent dates.

Ingredients

½ cup olive oil

One 8-ounce container yogurt

1 lemon, juiced

3 garlic cloves, minced

1 large shallot, minced

1 teaspoon ground cinnamon

1 teaspoon ground cardamom

½ teaspoon ground cloves

1 teaspoon salt

Pinch white pepper

2 pounds boneless leg of lamb, trimmed and cut into 1¼ inch cubes

24 fresh dates

Preparation

Serves 6

1. Combine oil, yogurt, lemon juice, garlic, shallot, cinnamon, cardamom, cloves, salt, and pepper in a large bowl. Mix thoroughly.
2. Add lamb to bowl and massage marinade into meat. Cover and refrigerate 4-24 hours.
3. Heat grill to hot.
4. Thread lamb and dates alternately onto six 12 inch metal skewers. Begin and end with lamb.
5. Grill kabobs, uncovered, 8 minutes for medium. Turn skewers one quarter every 2 minutes to ensure even browning. Adjust grill time for desired doneness.
6. To serve, slide lamb and dates onto individual platters.

Dates
Dates have been a staple food in both the Middle East and the Indus Valley for thousands of years and are mentioned in the Bible and the Quran. *Charoset*, a mixture that sometimes includes dates, walnuts, and wine, appears on the Passover Seder plate. When Muslims break the fast during Ramadan, it is traditional to first eat a date. They can be eaten fresh, dried, squeezed into juice, or dried and ground into flour.

Mahmudiye (Braised Chicken with Grapes)

Recipes for Mahmudiye *appear in records from 16th century Turkish Palace kitchens. This surprisingly simple preparation yields a subtly sweet and succulent chicken dish, perfect with your favorite pilaf.*

Ingredients

2 ounces dried apricots

1 cup boiling water

2 tablespoons butter

2 pounds boneless skinless chicken, cut into 1½ inch chunks

½ cup previously frozen pearl onions, patted dry

1 cup small seedless grapes

1 cup chicken broth

2 tablespoons honey

1 stick cinnamon

½ teaspoon salt

⅛ teaspoon fresh black pepper

2 tablespoons fresh lemon juice

Preparation

Serves 4

1. Place apricots in a shallow bowl and cover with boiling water. Allow to soak 1 hour then drain, pat dry, and julienne.
2. Melt the butter over medium heat in a large lidded saucepan. Add the chicken and sauté 3 minutes.
3. Add the onions and grapes and sauté 2 minutes.
4. Add the broth, honey, cinnamon, salt, and pepper. Bring to a boil, then reduce heat to medium-low. Cover and cook 30 minutes or until chicken is tender.
5. Uncover, remove the cinnamon, stir in lemon juice, and bring just to a boil. Serve piping hot.

Beet and Yogurt Salad

Roasting beets concentrates their flavors and takes the trouble out of peeling. When beets are combined with the creamy yogurt dressing, this vibrant and healthful salad adds visual appeal to your table.

Ingredients

6 medium beets, stems removed

1 clove garlic, minced

3 tablespoons chopped fresh mint

2 tablespoons fresh lemon juice

¼ cup olive oil

1 cup plain whole milk yogurt

Salt and pepper to taste

Preparation

Serves 6

1. Preheat oven to 375 degrees.
2. Wrap beets in aluminum foil. Bake 1 ½ hours.
3. Remove from oven and cool in foil 30 minutes. Slip off skin. Trim off ends and julienne.
4. Combine mint, lemon juice, oil, and yogurt in large bowl.
5. Fold in beets to coat with dressing. Chill.
6. Adjust seasoning. Serve.

Albaloo Polo (Rice with Black Cherry)

A Persian classic, this version of pilaf is sometimes called "Jeweled Rice," referring to the lovely bits of cherries and other fruits that are baked with the rice. It is a recipe that demands attention, but the result is an aromatic show-stopper worthy of every minute spent in preparation.

Ingredients

2 ½ cups basmati rice, rinsed well

1 ½ tablespoon salt

2 quarts water

½ cup butter, melted

1 small russet potato, peeled and thinly sliced

½ cup olive oil

1 cup dried cherries

2 tablespoons finely chopped walnuts

1 tablespoon raisins

1 tablespoon finely chopped dried apricots

½ teaspoon saffron threads, crushed

Preparation

1. Combine rice, salt, and water in a large wide non-stick saucepan and bring to a boil. Cook 8-10 minutes, stirring occasionally.
2. Strain rice and rinse with lukewarm water.
3. Add ¼ cup melted butter and 2 tablespoons of water to the same pot in which the rice was cooked.
4. Coat potato slices with ½ cup olive oil. Arrange potato slices in a single layer on the bottom of the pot, over the butter-water mixture.
5. Spoon half of the rice back in the pot, forming a mound. Sprinkle with cherries, walnuts, raisins, and apricots.
6. Cover with remaining rice. Distribute evenly into a conical shape.
7. Using the round handle of a wooden spoon, poke steam holes vertically into rice mound, all the way to the bottom of the pot. Drizzle the rest of melted butter evenly over the rice. Sprinkle with saffron.
8. Put a clean cotton dishtowel over the saucepan. Cover with the lid so that the cloth is held tightly over the rice cone to absorb steam while cooking. Fold the towel corners up over the top of the lid, protected from the flame.
9. Steam 15 minutes over medium heat. Lower heat and steam very slowly for 35-40 minutes.
10. Remove the lid and cloth. Carefully spoon out rice onto serving platter.
11. Use a spatula to loosen and remove crust from bottom of pot and place it on its own serving plate, golden side up.

Serves 8

Saffron
First cultivated in Greece, the flowering crocus is depicted in wall paintings from Bronze Age Thera, modern Santorini. Saffron is by weight the most expensive spice in the world, equal to truffles. It is an essential ingredient in Spanish *paella*.

Saffron Rice Pilaf

The palace kitchens of the Ottoman Turks were so vast that cooks specialized in preparing just one category of food. Pilaf was a category unto itself. This glorious fragrant dish is so beautiful and delicious, it hardly needs an accompaniment.

Ingredients

1 teaspoon saffron

2 tablespoons hot water

2 tablespoons butter

1 small onion, minced

1 cup basmati rice

¼ teaspoon ground cumin

¼ teaspoon ground cinnamon

1 pinch ground mace

1 pinch ground cloves

2 ½ cups beef, chicken, or vegetable broth

½ teaspoon salt

¼ teaspoon pepper

¼ cup slivered blanched almonds

¼ cup currants

Preparation

Serves 6

1. Soften saffron in hot water in small bowl.
2. Sauté onion in butter until golden. Add rice and toast, 2-3 minutes.
3. Add cumin, cinnamon, mace, and cloves. Stir for one minute.
4. Add broth and saffron, and bring to a boil. Cover. Reduce to low simmer and cook 20 minutes.
5. Fluff rice and stir in salt, pepper, almonds, and currants. Serve.

Pomegranate Apple Ice

The beautiful pomegranate is used widely across the Middle East. Its tart juice is a powerful source of vitamin C. This easy and refreshing dessert is a great project for the young cooks in your household. Grape jelly can be substituted for apple, according to availability.

Ingredients

3 cups pomegranate juice

¾ cup apple jelly

½ cup sugar

1 cup water

Preparation

Serves 4-6

1. Bring jelly, sugar, and water to a boil in a 2 quart saucepan. Stir until sugar is dissolved and thin syrup forms. Cool.
2. Stir pomegranate juice into syrup. Transfer mixture into 9x13" metal pan.
3. Put in freezer. Every 30 minutes, rake mixture with a fork to break up large chunks of ice. Continue until mixture is firm but not frozen.

Artifact

MESCALERO APACHE BASKET

New Mexico

ca. 1900–1918 CE

Native America

Blessed with a richly fertile land that sustained an astounding variety of foods—more, in fact, than it does today—the Native peoples of North America ate what they could find, kill, or grow. Although corn, squash, and beans—called the "Three Sisters" because they can be grown together to benefit all three—were staple foods in many regions, local diets depended on the weather, the indigenous flora and fauna, soil conditions, and the exigencies of the seasons. Summer brought berries and wild onions; fall, nuts and pumpkins. The Hopi woman of the Southwest ground corn to make *piki* bread. The Penobscot fisherman on the coast of Maine fed on oysters, clams, and lobsters boiled in seawater. Blackfoot, Crow, and Pawnee hunters of the Great Plains killed bison, elk, and moose. The Ojibwe peoples of the Great Lakes harvested wild rice. From the earliest times, although each region offered its specialties, most Native American peoples practiced both hunting and gathering as well as some form of agriculture.

In the Southwest, corn was sacred. To the Navajo, the Hopi, the Zuni, and the Pueblo, the corn plant was as close a relative as a child; a good man or woman is nurturing of both crops and children, thereby linking garden plots to family harmony. Corn was ground into flour for bread. In domestic religious rites, it was common for a family to share a drink made from corn. The emergence of the new corn crop signified a spiritual beginning, symbolizing prosperity and hope. Other plants grown in this dry land were pumpkins, sunflowers, and red and green peppers, which were cooked over a slow burning fire to make chili, to which mutton was added after the Spanish introduced sheep to the Americas in the 16th century. Less common delicacies were the cactus, prickly pear, and sumpweed.

The Northwest had an entirely different climate and bioregion where the Chinook, the Tillamook, and the Tlingit were largely hunters and gatherers. Birds' eggs, waterfowl, bear and seal meat, venison, rabbit, and all manner of berries were eaten. However, fishing was their mainstay. Unlike most other hunting/gathering societies which must

Mescalero Apache Basket
Coiled of sumac and yucca plant fibers, the design of this basket is in the form of a four-petal flower with stepped triangles near the rim.
Museum object #NA8779

be nomadic to follow their food sources, the natives of the Northwest received from the great rivers abundant supplies of salmon. This enabled more permanent settlements, craft specialization, and the beginnings of social stratification. Complex fishing methods developed from the earliest times. Petroglyphs and pictographs depict weirs, nets, traps of twigs and branches, and countless types of hooks to catch the salmon as they fought their way upstream to breed. On large wooden platforms, built out into the Columbia River, fishermen would snare the fish, which were then rubbed with spices—mint, licorice root, or soaked and minced pine needles—then wrapped in leaves and grilled or pit roasted. To preserve their catch for the winter months, fish was dried in the sun or over fires, salted, or sometimes frozen. In this region *potlatches* or gift-giving ceremonies lasted several days, perhaps in honor of a birth, a naming, a wedding, or a death. Much feasting, dancing, and singing ensued. Fish and seal meat was shared and eaten in abundance; a special delicacy was the *gumboot chiton*, a giant orange mollusk, found along the shores of the northern Pacific. These mollusks can be harvested only once a year, which adds to their rarity and desirability. Today, gumboots are steamed and frozen, so are enjoyed all year.

On the Great Plains, among the Blackfoot, Crow, and Cheyenne, meat was a staple. Small game—deer, rabbit, and antelope—was hunted until the Spaniards introduced horses, making possible the round ups of big game that were driven over cliffs to their deaths. Bison provided meat, clothing, and bones for tools. Meat was eaten raw or boiled, sometimes placed in the stomach of a bison, which was then eaten along with the stew within. To preserve the large amount of meat that was killed in a successful hunt, it was dried until brittle, in the sun or over a fire, pounded with dried berries into a powder, and mixed with melted fat. The result, called *pemmican*, lasted for months. As in the Northwest, people of the Great Plains held to the belief that to maintain political authority, wealth, including food, should be shared, a practice that continues in some measure in powwows today.

The North Atlantic coast with 6,000 miles of shoreline provided the Narragansetts, the Micmacs, and the Mohegans with fish and shellfish. The inland forests offered small game, berries, and nuts (hickory, walnut, chestnut, acorn, and hazel). The Algonquins first processed the sap of the maple tree into syrup. Wild turkeys abounded though

Artifact

ARCTIC CHAR CARVING
Quebec, Canada
1975

Artic Char Carving
Created by the Inuit people, this soapstone carving of an arctic char reflects the culture's longstanding reliance on aquatic life as a source of nourishment. Museum object #2012-25-7

Ancestral Pueblo Ceramic Ladle
Painted in the Tularosa Black-on-White style, this ladle is decorated with lines and geometric forms. It was designed with a rattle in its handle and signed by "Maggie." Museum object #NA2202

Artifact

ANCESTRAL PUEBLO CERAMIC LADLE

Little Colorado River region, Arizona

ca. 1100–1250 CE

Artifact

ANCESTRAL HOPI BOWL

Sikyátki, Arizona

1400–1500 CE

they may or may not have been eaten at the first Thanksgiving. Rather more quickly than in remote areas, Native peoples in this region adapted foods and foodways from immigrants, although they maintained their traditional taste for clams from present day New Brunswick and Maine, beach plums from Cape Cod, crabs and oysters from Maryland, blueberries from the New Jersey Pine Barrens, and the ubiquitous maize.

Southeastern peoples—the Cherokee, the Creek, and the Seminole—were both farmers and hunter/gatherers, enjoying an especially rich and varied diet. Corn, used to make grits, hominy, and fermented liquors (still popular as bourbon), was and still is the main staple of southern cooking. Other cultivated crops were beans, squash, sunflowers, and sunchokes (Jerusalem artichokes). All sorts of small game were hunted, including wild turkeys, partridge, quail, ducks, pigeons, rabbits, squirrels, beavers, otters, and raccoons. Berries—cranberries, blueberries, elderberries, huckleberries, gooseberries, and juniper berries—were eaten raw or boiled with honey and vinegar to produce sauces for meats. Inland rivers and lakes supplied freshwater crayfish, and along the Gulf Coast, oysters, clams, mussels, crabs, turtles, and alligators were gathered or hunted.

Today, many North Americans from Native cultures eat foods obtained at their local supermarkets, while preserving a particular food that defines tribal identity and is honored in festivals that welcome the arrival of a new crop—the first corn, the first strawberries, the first salmon, even the first acorns. Through thousands of years, Native Americans, with ingenuity and hard work, took the bounties of this land and adapted them to their needs and tastes.

Artifact

POMO BASKET
California
Late 19th Century

Ancestral Hopi Bowl
The image on this hand-coiled Sikyátki polychrome bowl has been described by Hopi artists living today as a human hand catching the rain bird. Museum object #39051

Pomo Basket
This shallow boat-shaped basket from the Pomo culture in Upper Lake California is made of willow, sedge root, and bullrush root fibers and decorated with feathers, clam shells, and glass beads. Museum object #NA7871

The Three Sisters

Corn, beans, and squash—the three sisters—are the most common ingredients in the diets of Native Americans. All are indigenous to the Americas and have been under cultivation here since at least 6000 BCE. That they were planted together, supporting the needs of each, was an agricultural innovation seen as a major contribution to horticulture. Corn seeds are first planted in a raised mound; some Eastern tribes place a dead fish in the mound as fertilizer. Once the corn sprouts, beans and squash are seeded around its base. As the corn grows, it provides support for the beans to climb. The squash grows around the base, holding moisture and acting as a ground cover to inhibit weeds.

The three sisters also support one another nutritionally. The corn needs nitrogen to flourish. The beans capture nitrogen as they mature, thereby enriching the soil. Squash provides vitamins and minerals. And the three sisters combine to make a balanced meal. Though Native Americans did not understand the biochemical foundation of the three sisters' relationship, their close observation of the natural world and their deep understanding of man's place among its gifts is evident in the high esteem given to the three sisters. Plantings were honored by family and community ceremonies that enhanced social and sacred bonds. These practices are still observed among descendants of Native Americans from the southwest to the northeast. Recently, home gardeners have adopted this companion planting technique and champion it for efficiency and sustainability.

Adding to the success and popularity of the three sisters planting technique is the opportunity to choose varieties of corn, beans, and squash that best suit site, climate, and taste. Pole beans, green beans, or peas work equally well. Choose zucchini or crookneck, patty pan or pumpkin. Any combination will make a fine succotash.

Hopi Seed Jar
Collected by ethnologist Stuart Culin on the Wanamaker Expedition to the Southwest in 1901, this jar was painted in the Sikyátki Polychrome style. It is decorated with squash blossoms, dragonflies, and ears of corn. Museum object #29-77-703

Artifact

HOPI SEED JAR

Arizona

ca. 1400–1625 CE

Recipes

Lobster, Corn, and
Fingerling Chowder
(pictured)

Clam Fritters

Roasted Salmon
Fillets with Caviar
and Nut Oil

Buffalo Steaks
with Juniper and
Blackberry Sauce

Wild Rice Salad with
Fruit and Nuts

Acorn Squash
with Black Walnuts

Fresh Corn and Lima
Succotash

Sunchoke Mash

Blue Corn
Pancakes

Cranberry Jam

Photo: © Jennifer Yu, 2013

Lobster, Corn, and Fingerling Chowder

This luscious chowder is grand enough for center stage. With a crispy green salad and a side of hot corn bread, you and your guests will want for nothing else. Well, perhaps a nice glass of very dry Riesling.

Ingredients

3 slices bacon, diced

1 onion, chopped

3 ears fresh corn, kernels removed

2 celery stalks, diced

1 pound fingerling potatoes cut into ½ inch pieces

1 cup fish stock

One 8-ounce bottle clam juice

½ cup white wine

2 cups heavy cream

1 pound lobster meat, cooked and cut into 1 inch chunks

1 tablespoon fresh thyme, chopped

1 tablespoon fresh chives, chopped

Salt and pepper to taste

Preparation

Serves 6

1. Brown bacon bits in a large soup pot or Dutch oven.
2. Add onion, corn kernels, and celery. Sauté over medium low 4-5 minutes until tender.
3. Add potatoes, stock, clam juice, and wine. Bring to a boil. Reduce to a simmer and cook, covered, for 15 minutes or until potatoes are tender.
4. Add heavy cream and bring to a low boil.
5. Add lobster, thyme, and chives. Cook over medium heat until lobster is heated through, 2-3 minutes.
6. Taste for seasoning and add salt and pepper as desired. Serve immediately.

Lobster
The North American lobster did not achieve popularity until the mid-19th century. Prior to this time, lobster was used as fertilizer or as fish bait, or it was thought of as food for the poor, for indentured servants, or for prison inmates. Today, lobster is known for being one of the most expensive types of seafood.

Clam Fritters

Fresh clams really matter in this dish. The canned variety is too salty and their texture is often mushy. So take the time to steam a couple pounds of Littlenecks or Cherrystones. You will appreciate the result. These make a great starter for a casual meal or a sports party.

Ingredients

1 cup shelled clams

¼ cup reserved clam juice

½ cup all purpose flour

½ cup finely ground cornmeal or corn flour

1 teaspoon baking powder

1 large egg, beaten

½ cup minced scallion

¼ teaspoon salt

¼ teaspoon pepper

Corn oil for frying

Preparation

Serves 15

1. Combine 2 tablespoons clam juice, flour, corn meal, baking powder, and egg to make a smooth batter.
2. Add clams, remaining clam juice, scallions, salt, and pepper. Combine well.
3. Heat 2 inches of oil in a saucepan to 375 degrees.
4. Drop heaping tablespoons of batter into oil. Cook 5-6 minutes, turning to brown on all sides. Do not crowd pan and cook in batches if necessary.
5. Remove fritters to drain on a rack, sprinkle with additional salt. Serve hot.

Roasted Salmon Fillets with Caviar and Nut Oil

This is a simple yet elegant preparation for the ubiquitous salmon fillet. Of course you could forgo the caviar, but the presentation would suffer and you would miss those delightful salty bites of salmon delicacy.

Ingredients

Four 6-to 8-ounce center-cut salmon fillets, 1½ inches thick, skin on

¼ cup hazelnut or walnut oil

1 tablespoon salt

2 shallots, minced

½ cup dry white wine

1 small jar salmon caviar

Preparation

Serves 4

1. Preheat oven to 425 degrees.
2. Pat fillets dry, check for bones, and coat lightly with oil.
3. Place fillets in shallow baking dish. Sprinkle with salt, remaining oil, and shallots. Pour wine around fillets.
4. Roast 10 minutes. Check for doneness. Continue roasting until fish flakes easily.
5. Remove to serving platter. Pour any remaining pan juices over the fish and top with caviar.

Buffalo Steaks with Juniper and Blackberry Sauce

Buffalo is gaining in popularity as a leaner and more nutritious alternative to beef, and is increasingly available in local supermarkets. This preparation is perhaps one of the most flavorful meat dishes you will ever serve. The sauce is rich, complex, and beautiful and would be equally delectable served with grilled or roasted venison.

Ingredients

4 boneless 1 inch thick buffalo strip steaks, about 6 ounces each

Salt and pepper to taste

2 tablespoons corn oil

2 tablespoons juniper berries, crushed

1 tablespoon fennel seed, crushed

1 tomato, diced

1 small carrot, diced

1 small onion, diced

½ cup red wine

2 cups beef stock

1 tablespoon honey

1 tablespoon cider vinegar

1 cup fresh or frozen blackberries

Preparation

Serves 4

1. Place steaks on a tray and sprinkle both sides with salt and pepper. Cover with plastic wrap, and hold at room temperature while preparing sauce.
2. Heat oil in a medium saucepan and sauté juniper and fennel seed until fragrant.
3. Add tomato, carrot, and onion and cook over medium heat, stirring constantly, until browned.
4. Add wine. Bring to a boil, reduce to a simmer, and cook until reduced in half, about 10 minutes.
5. Add stock, honey, vinegar, and blackberries. Boil vigorously for 5 minutes.
6. Reduce to a simmer and cook, stirring frequently, until sauce is reduced and thickened to the consistency of heavy cream. Strain, pressing on solids to release juices. Return sauce to pan, and take pan off the heat.
7. Heat a grill, grill pan, or cast iron skillet to high and sear steaks, about 3 minutes per side for medium rare. Remove to a platter to rest, lightly tented with foil, 5 minutes.
8. Heat sauce over medium heat, just to a simmer.
9. Slice each steak against the grain into ½ inch slices.
10. Spoon some sauce on each plate, top with steak slices, and serve additional sauce on the side.

Blackberries
Because blackberries can be harvested for only three weeks during the year, usually starting at the beginning of July, their fresh market presence is limited. They grow wild in North America, especially in the Northwest, and contain less sugar and more fiber than most other berries.

Wild Rice Salad with Fruit and Nuts

We sometimes forget that wild rice is native to North America and has been harvested by Native Americans throughout history. Be sure to purchase the authentic grain, preferably one grown in Minnesota or Wisconsin. This hearty side dish is as nutritious as it is beautiful. It works especially well with roasted turkey, squab, or quail.

Ingredients

1 cup raw wild rice, rinsed

6 cups vegetable stock

½ cup pecans, chopped

½ cup walnuts, chopped

½ cup currants

½ cup prunes, chopped

1 orange, zested and juiced

1 shallot, sliced very thin

¼ cup walnut oil

1 tablespoon marjoram, chopped

1 tablespoon thyme, chopped

1 teaspoon salt

Preparation

Serves 6-8

1. Bring rice and stock to a boil in a large saucepan. Reduce to simmer and cook, 45-55 minutes, until rice is very tender. Drain. Place in large mixing bowl.

2. Add remaining ingredients to cooked rice. Toss well. Cover and let stand 2-3 hours. Serve at room temperature.

Wild Rice
Wild rice plants grow in shallow water in small lakes and slow-moving streams in North America. Often only the flowering head of the plant rises above the water. Native Americans and others harvested wild rice by canoeing into a stand of plants, bending the ripe grain heads with wooden sticks called knockers, and threshing the seeds into their canoes.

Acorn Squash with Black Walnuts

The maple-walnut flavor of the simple filling permeates the succulent flesh of the squash and makes this a go-to recipe for a fall or winter menu. Common walnuts could be substituted but never compromise on maple syrup!

Ingredients

3 acorn squash

½ cup pure maple syrup

3 tablespoons butter, at room temperature

3 tablespoons finely chopped black walnuts

¼ teaspoon salt

Preparation

Serves 6

1. Preheat oven to 350 degrees.
2. Cut squash in half, lengthwise, and remove seeds.
3. Mix syrup, butter, black walnuts, and salt to form a paste.
4. Place squash in baking dish and place a dollop of maple paste in each.
5. Bake 45 minutes or until lightly browned and fork tender.

Fresh Corn and Lima Succotash

This is a quick and easy natural combination of ingredients that are often grown together. Variations have been served for centuries. It is delicious when all ingredients are at the peak of their summer freshness so save it for your July and August menus. It pairs especially well with a simple roast chicken or grilled pork chops.

Ingredients

1 cup freshly shelled lima beans

2 cups fresh corn kernels (cut from 3-4 ears)

1 shallot, sliced thin

1 medium zucchini or yellow squash, diced

2 tablespoons butter

2 tablespoons chopped fresh chives

Salt and pepper to taste

Preparation

Serves 6

1. Bring ½ inch of water to boil in small saucepan.
2. Add lima beans. Cover. Lower heat and steam beans 10-15 minutes until just tender. Drain and set aside.
3. Sauté corn, shallot, and squash in butter, 3-5 minutes, until corn and squash are crisp tender.
4. Add lima beans, salt, and pepper. Stir to combine.
5. Serve sprinkled with chives.

Sunchoke Mash

Sunchokes are native to North America and are of the same family as the sunflower. They are not artichokes at all. Available in the spring, they provide a less starchy variation on our beloved mashed potatoes. You can vary the seasonings in this dish to suit your taste but do not skip the half and half.

Ingredients

2 pounds sunchokes (Jerusalem artichokes), scrubbed well

1 pound baking potatoes, peeled

2 teaspoons salt

½ teaspoon chili powder

2 cups half and half

2 tablespoons butter at room temperature

¼ teaspoon black pepper

¼ cup fresh parsley leaves, roughly chopped

Preparation

Serves 6

1. Cut sunchokes and potato into 1 inch pieces.
2. Place sunchokes, potatoes, salt, chili powder, and half and half into a large pot. Add enough water to cover. Bring to a simmer.
3. Simmer gently for 20-30 minutes, until tender. Drain.
4. Return sunchokes and potatoes to pot. Add butter. Mash with a hand held masher. Add pepper to taste.
5. Transfer to a serving bowl and garnish with parsley. Add an extra dab of butter and a sprinkle of salt to taste.

Sunchokes

The sunchoke is a species of sunflower native to eastern North America. It is also known as the Jerusalem artichoke although it has no connection with Jerusalem and is not an artichoke. Cultivated for its tuber which is used as a root vegetable, a sunchoke looks like a small, knobby potato but is crunchier and sweeter and tastes slightly like an artichoke.

Blue Corn Pancakes

This is a nod to the sacred Piki Bread of the Hopi. Yellow or white cornmeal may be substituted if blue is unavailable, but the visual result is just not as much fun. Paired with cranberry jam, these pancakes make a great brunch offering. They are perfect Sunday supper fare as well.

| Ingredients | Preparation | Serves 4 |

Ingredients

½ cup all purpose flour

1 cup blue cornmeal

1 tablespoon sugar

2 teaspoons baking powder

½ teaspoon sea salt

2 large eggs, beaten

1¼ cup buttermilk

2 tablespoons corn oil

Preparation   **Serves 4**

1. Heat a griddle or non-stick skillet over medium heat.
2. Combine dry ingredients in a mixing bowl. In a separate bowl, combine eggs and milk.
3. Add milk mixture to dry ingredients all at once. Stir to combine.
4. Add corn oil to hot skillet. Swirl to distribute.
5. Ladle batter into hot pan forming individual pancakes. Using a large spatula, turn when bubbles appear on surface. Cook approximately 2 minutes per side.
6. Serve hot with butter and cranberry jam.

Cranberry Jam

The vanilla gives this condiment a surprising depth of flavor. The result is as beautiful as it is tasty.

Ingredients

1 vanilla bean, halved lengthwise

One 12-ounce bag cranberries

1 cup sugar

½ cup honey

¼ cup lemon juice

½ cup water

Pinch salt

Preparation   **Yield** 2 cups

1. Scrape vanilla seeds into a 2 quart saucepan.
2. Add remaining ingredients. Bring to a boil.
3. Reduce to simmer and cook 20 minutes, stirring constantly. Mixture should be thick.
4. Press through a sieve to remove solids.
5. Cover and refrigerate up to one week.

Artifact

**UMBRO-ETRUSCAN
TERRACOTTA VOTIVE SET**
Todi (north of Rome), Italy
3rd century BCE

Rome

The first Romans hunted in the dense Apennine forests, where wolves and bears were their rivals. They cultivated small grain plots outside their town walls, fished in the Tiber River, and ate what they killed, grew, or caught—no pasta, no artichokes, and no gelato yet. In fact, the nature of the early Roman's diet lasted throughout the many "Romes" that came after the city's founding in 753 BCE: its hearty simplicity, even poverty, registers with Republican Romans as an attribute of the stern "plain living" that helped them build a mighty state. In later times, we still note the significance of pork, brought to the city from the herds of pigs roaming Apulia; of bread, made from cereal grains such as emmer, spelt, and barley; of honey, gathered in the hills; and of the apples and pears from the first cultivated orchards.

In the early Imperial period, Romans changed what they ate as their world changed, due to trade with larger, more sophisticated regions and more land under cultivation. From the 1st century CE a cookery book, called *Apicius* after a notable gourmet of generations before, included recipes arranged in chapters like a modern cookbook; it detailed every step in the preparation of dishes favored by the wealthy such as roast kid or lamb stew.

Consumption of wine also increased. Borrowing techniques from the Etruscans and Greeks, Romans seized on grape-growing and wine-making with enthusiasm. Working people drank wine (likely the rawest and most adulterated of the vintage) with their morning porridge of millet and beans; the middle class drank wine with their mackerel and cheese at noon; the senatorial class ate a main meal in the mid-afternoon, accompanied by wine that was carefully chosen by region and grape, and watered much more lightly. For much of the Republican Era, women were required to abstain from wine, but by the Common Era this prohibition was abandoned.

Umbro-Etruscan Terracotta Votive Set
This offering tray holds a collection of miniature food: fish, chicken, bread, vegetables, and fruit. A small pitcher completes the set.
Museum object #MS1407-1423 and MS1425-1427

Too much display at meals was still frowned upon, of course. Petronius's satirical novel on the excesses of the *nouveau riche* has a chapter, "Trimalchio's Dinner," that describes dishes like roast flamingo—maybe not so tasty but certainly rare and expensive! The senatorial, land-holding upper class, on the other hand, used tasteful gifts of food from their own villa-farms to knit together power blocks and families. They would send off ducks with rainbow plumage or a giant sturgeon caught that morning and rushed to town. Food was for them not just an assertion of wealth. It celebrated the connection of the ruling class to the abundant earth. In villa after villa, over the centuries of the Empire, mosaic floors spread underfoot the bounty of the harvest and the endless gifts of the sea. The mosaic inscription *Sume*, translated as "Take," offers these most important riches to the gracious host and his or her guests.

At the height of Imperial power, foodstuffs poured into Rome, chiefly by sea: olive oil from Spain and North Africa, wine from the south of Italy and the Eastern Mediterranean, grain from Egypt (until Constantine split the empire in 330 CE and Egypt's grain went to Constantinople) and North Africa, considered the breadbasket of Rome. The thousands of broken *amphorae* (earthenware jars) that form Monte Testaccio, below the Aventine Hill, were discarded after their loads of oil and wine were distributed—part of the *annona civica*, a ration of grain, oil, wine, and often pork and honey that was given to each Roman citizen by law. Woe to the consul of the year when bad weather sank the ships from the south, or the harvests in North Africa failed; he could have his house burned around him or be beaten by angry citizens.

Even comparatively modest citizens, however, were now eating a more varied and interesting diet than had their distant forebears. In the sludge of the lava-blocked sewers of Pompeii, archaeologists have identified remnants of lentils, apples, anchovies, sea bream, mackerel, barley, dill, and poppy seeds. We know less about the simpler but charming villas with dining rooms cooled by the film of water over a mosaic, with benches arranged in a semi-circle like an indoor picnic. Dining together cemented friendships and alliances, and diners valued good conversation and temperate eating and drinking.

Artifact

ROMAN BRONZE JUG
Karanog, Nubia
(northern Sudan)
3rd century CE

Roman Bronze Jug
This bronze vessel has a trefoil mouth and the handle is decorated with human forms. It was excavated during the 1907–1910 Eckley B. Coxe Expedition to Nubia. Museum object #E7512

Limestone Loculus Cover
A reclining youth holds a vase in his left hand on this loculus or burial chamber cover. The youth is accompanied by two smaller figures—perhaps slaves—who hold an amphora and a cup. The rigidity of their poses is typical of Roman art in Syria. Museum object #CBS8902

Artifact

LIMESTONE LOCULUS COVER

Palmyra, Syria

2nd century CE

Artifact

RIBBED FLASK

Mediterranean

Late 4th century CE

Then the Empire contracted. Though for centuries Rome maintained itself as one of the centers of the Western Empire, finally, when its power dwindled and new kingdoms ruled its outer regions, Rome's food chain was shortened. People left; the population dropped to a few thousand. It took 800 years for Italy to be reinvented as a cluster of dukedoms and free cities, jostling for control of the growing trade to the East and from the north of Europe. Rome was for years a very dry bone fought over by local families, but by the late 15th century the Pope, after schisms and exiles lasting for centuries, was established as a temporal prince over the Papal States.

As a Renaissance state, Rome swept its streets, built palaces and churches, and imported some good cooks from its rivals, especially Florence and Milan. Food was as much a part of the display necessary to a Renaissance prince as were collections of antiquities and marble-walled receiving rooms. There were new delicacies like corn, tomatoes, and peppers from the Spanish colonies of the Western Hemisphere; sugar, almonds, and spinach from the Arab world: princely kitchens produced a myriad of dishes presented to be admired. Flavors were varied and subtle; the tables were decorated with gold and silver services. Methods of preparation and presentation were sophisticated: marinating, fermenting, baking, broiling, and steaming produced a series of colorful dishes at a dinner of the Roman elite. When Catherine de' Medici married the heir to the French throne, she took her cook with her; France is said to owe its cuisine (and ice cream) to her Italian tastes.

This cuisine of the upper class filtered down, as it always does, to the mercantile and craft guild classes. Simplified and streamlined, it crops up in specialty shops and Roman *ristoranti* today: gelato, variations on sauces, and the attention to freshness in greens and vegetables. Wheat retains its centuries-old dominance; no Roman meal lacks bread, even when it is complementing a first course of pasta. And the Roman devotion to pork has lasted from those Iron Age boar hunters to the contemporary workman buying *porchetta* from a street vendor. The fresh wines of the Roman hills, the *Colli Albani* and *Frascati*, and the bitter greens of the first spring salads remind 21st century Romans— as they did the frugal housekeeper in Republican Rome—of the long compact between Rome and the abundance and importance of food.

Artifact

ROMAN SPICE JAR
Beth Shean, Israel
4th century CE

Ribbed Flask
With its fine decoration and elaborate loop handle, this glass *oinochoe* or flask might have been used at the table. Museum object #MS5494

Roman Spice Jar
This green and blue glass jar probably contained spices, which were used to enhance a bland dish.
Museum object #MS4933A

Wine

Fermenting grapes into wine began in the Near East and China around 10,000 years ago and later spread across Europe and Asia. By about 2300 BCE, Crete adopted similar techniques for making wine. Canaanites and Phoenicians (and later Greeks) introduced viticulture to Sicily and southern Italy between 800 and 700 BCE. With its long shoreline and mild climate, Italy proved so hospitable to the growth of wine grapes that the Greeks nicknamed it "Oenotria" or land of wine.

The Etruscans, inhabitants of central Italy from *ca.* 800 BCE until, beginning in the 4th century BCE, they were assimilated by the Romans, improved the techniques introduced by Greek colonists by burying the fermenting crushed grapes in clay containers called *pithoi,* which were stored in deep, cool cellars. Excavated archaeological evidence such as pottery sherds and grape seeds suggest that by *ca.* 300 BCE, the Romans, who had earlier drunk mead or beer, turned enthusiastically to wine. This transition was aided by a theft from the Carthaginians of a book on winemaking, which was translated into Latin and made available in Italy.

The Romans improved pressing techniques, resulting in a better wine, by storing it for longer periods in sealed *amphorae.* They also studied soil preferences and the arts of pruning and irrigation. Because Roman wine was high in alcohol content and was particularly acidic, it was mixed with honey, herbs, and spices; chalk to reduce its acidity; and water—sometimes sea water. An especially good wine from the Naples area was Falerian; it was so favored that Caligula (reigned 37–41 CE) fed it to his horse. As the empire grew, wine was exported in large airtight wooden barrels, perhaps of Celtic invention, and knowledge of winemaking spread as far as present day France and England.

Today, Italy produces nearly 1,500 varieties of wine. From Piedmont in the north comes the dry, rosy Barolos; from Tuscany, the full-bodied Brunellos; and from Sicily, the rich, sweet Marsalas. In the 19th and early 20th centuries, Italian wine was primarily known for its low cost until in the 1960s regulations were tightened and wines were classified for quality, giving Italy's greatest vintages new dignity in the world of wine connoisseurship.

Graeco-Roman Wine Amphora
Large ceramic amphorae were used in the transport of wine. This encrusted amphora was found on a Mediterranean shipwreck by underwater explorer Jacques Cousteau. Museum object #89-2-4

Artifact

**GRAECO-ROMAN
WINE AMPHORA**

Grand Congloué, France
(near Marseilles)
110–80 BCE

Recipes

Carciofi alla Guida
Crispy Fried Artichokes

Asparagus Frittata

Fennel and Orange
Salad

Creamy
Herbed Polenta

Vermicelli with
Calamari and Shrimp

Grilled Steak,
Tuscan Style
(pictured)

Vitello Tonnato
Veal in Tuna Sauce

Sautéed
Broccoli Rabe with
Caper Berries

Farro and Green Bean
Salad

Pignoli Cookies

Carciofi alla Giudia *(Crispy Fried Artichokes)*

This classic Roman preparation is all about the perfect ingredients and deft preparation. Make it in the spring when baby artichokes are in the market. Use the egg-sized purple variety if you can find them. The quality of the olive oil really makes a difference and a deep-fat thermometer is critical. Warning: these will be eaten as fast as you make them so you may want to double the recipe!

Ingredients

2 lemons

18 baby artichokes, purple preferred

Salt and pepper

4 cups extra virgin olive oil

Preparation

Serves 6

1. Fill large bowl with cold water. Add juice of 1 lemon.
2. Cut stems off artichokes, flush with base. Bend back outer leaves until they snap off closer to base. Remove several layers of leaves in the same manner until exposed leaves are tender. If baby artichokes are very fresh and tender, you will not need to remove many leaves.
3. Cut off tough tips of leaves with kitchen shears.
4. Spread leaves and remove choke, if present. Place in lemon water until ready to fry.
5. Heat oil in a wide deep pan until deep-fat thermometer reads 300 degrees.
6. Place artichokes on a clean towel, stem ends up. Press to spread leaves and remove water. Turn artichokes over and sprinkle with salt and pepper.
7. Using long-handled tongs, submerge artichokes in oil, stem side down, and simmer until tender, about 5-8 minutes. Artichokes should be crisp but not overly browned. Fry in batches if necessary to avoid crowding.
8. Remove with tongs. Drain on paper towels.

Artichokes
The artichoke is a variety of thistle that is native to the Mediterranean area where it grew wild. Disliked for its bitter taste and odor until late in the Roman period, and essentially forgotten after that until the Renaissance, it was finally rendered agreeable by being cooked with honey, bay leaves, lilies, or roses. The edible portions are the fleshy lower portions (the heart) and, of course, the lower parts of the leaves.

Asparagus Frittata

Asparagus was enjoyed by the ancient Egyptians and Greeks. It became a cash crop for the Venetians. It often has a prominent place at spring feasts celebrating Passover or Easter. The frittata, understood by most as Italy's version of an open faced crustless quiche, has appeared on menus and in cookbooks for about half a century. This simple preparation of high quality ingredients at the peak of freshness is absolutely delicious.

Ingredients

1 pound fresh asparagus

3 tablespoons butter, melted

¼ teaspoon salt

¼ teaspoon pepper

1 pinch grated nutmeg

1 pinch cinnamon

½ cup asiago cheese, grated

¾ cup shredded prosciutto ham

6 eggs beaten well with
  3 tablespoons heavy cream

3 tablespoons grated parmesan

Preparation

1. Preheat oven to 350 degrees.
2. Cut asparagus into 7 inch spears, discarding woody ends. Blanch 3 minutes in boiling water and plunge into ice water bath to stop cooking.
3. Pour melted butter into 8x8" baking dish and spread to cover bottom and sides.
4. Arrange drained asparagus spears in neat alternating layers. Sprinkle with salt, pepper, nutmeg, cinnamon, asiago, and prosciutto.
5. Pour egg mixture over asparagus. Sprinkle with parmesan.
6. Bake 30 minutes or until eggs are set and top is golden.

Serves 6

Pecorino Romano
Pecorino Romano is a hard Italian cheese, made of unpasturized ewe's milk. It is often grated on pastas or salads. It has been produced in the environs of Rome for about 2,000 years. It is described as aromatic, bold, briny, and peppery, and is especially delicious eaten with ripe summer pears, walnuts, and a drizzle of honey.

Fennel and Orange Salad

The flavors of fennel and citrus are a natural marriage. Both are common to the Mediterranean where variations of this simple clean salad abound. Blood oranges are a wonderful substitute when in season. Pink grapefruit works as well. An especially fine pecorino will make a noticeable difference.

Ingredients

3 medium fennel, trimmed and cored

1 lemon, juiced

½ cup olive oil

3 oranges, zested and segmented

3 ounces pecorino cheese, shaved with a vegetable peeler

½ teaspoon salt

¼ teaspoon pepper

Preparation

Serves 6

1. Using a mandolin, slice fennel very thin. Place in large bowl with lemon juice and oil. Cover and rest at room temperature 30 minutes.
2. Add orange segments, cheese, salt, and pepper. Toss lightly and serve with a sprinkle of orange zest.

Creamy Herbed Polenta

Corn was not available in the Old World until Columbus returned from the Americas. Thus the ancient Romans missed out on polenta, as we know it today. They did make a similar dish using available grains like millet. Once cornmeal arrived, there was no turning back. If you have come to think of polenta as a bland backdrop, this recipe will change your mind. Rich and flavorful, it is wonderful with a simple tomato sauce or aside a juicy veal chop.

Ingredients

2 quarts low-sodium vegetable broth

1 teaspoon salt

2 ¼ cups yellow corn meal, medium grind

¾ cup Parmesan cheese, grated

¼ cup chopped fresh herbs (combined rosemary, parsley, and oregano)

¼ teaspoon black pepper

4 tablespoons unsalted butter

½ cup heavy cream

Preparation

Serves 6-8

1. Bring stock and water to a boil in a large saucepan.
2. Slowly add cornmeal in a steady stream, stirring constantly over medium high heat.
3. When mixture bubbles, reduce heat to medium low and cook 10 minutes or until it begins to thicken, stirring constantly.
4. Slowly stir in cheese and all but 1 tablespoon of herbs. When well combined, whisk in pepper, butter, and cream.
5. Continue to cook, whisking constantly over medium low heat, until polenta pulls away from the sides of the pan.
6. Transfer to a warmed platter and serve topped with remaining herbs.

Vermicelli with Calamari and Shrimp

Like so many wonderful Mediterranean recipes, this one is a simple combination of fresh ingredients, prepared with minimal fuss. Garlic and a hint of red pepper enhance the flavor of the seafood. The butter and lemon provide a silky finish. Serve with a simple green salad and some crusty bread, and this is dinner in less than half an hour.

Ingredients

1 dozen fresh baby calamari, cleaned

½ cup olive oil

Pinch red pepper flakes

2 dozen medium shrimp, peeled and deveined

2 cloves garlic, minced

One 8-ounce bottle clam juice

½ cup fresh parsley

1 pound vermicelli

2 tablespoons butter

1 lemon, juiced

Preparation

Serves 6

1. Cut calamari bodies into 1/3 inch rings. Cut tentacles in half, lengthwise.
2. Heat oil in large skillet over medium high. Add red pepper flakes and cook 30 seconds.
3. Add calamari, shrimp, and garlic and sauté for 3-4 minutes, until shrimp turns pink and calamari are tender.
4. Add clam juice and bring to a simmer. Remove from heat and stir in parsley.
5. Cook vermicelli according to package directions. Drain, reserving 1 cup pasta water.
6. Add pasta to skillet with seafood sauce. Toss to combine. Add additional pasta water if necessary to keep sauce loose.
7. Swirl in butter and lemon juice to finish.

Grilled Steak, Tuscan Style

Here is a recipe for the grill master. All grilling derives from ancient techniques of roasting over open wood fires. This preparation, calling for a hefty 3-inch steak over a ripping hot flame, respects that history. Do not be tempted to modify this recipe. It is perfect just as it is.

Ingredients

2 tablespoons fresh rosemary, chopped

2 tablespoons fresh oregano, chopped

2 tablespoons salt

2 tablespoons black pepper

¼ cup extra virgin olive oil

1 T-bone steak, 3 inches thick (approximately 3 ½ pounds)

Coarse salt for seasoning

Extra virgin olive oil for finishing

Preparation

Serves 4

1. Combine rosemary, oregano, salt, pepper and oil in a blender and mix to create a paste.
2. Pat steak dry and coat with rub on both sides. Let rest at room temperature 30 minutes.
3. Preheat outdoor grill to high.
4. Grill 12 minutes on first side and turn to grill 9 minutes on second side. Steak will be charred and medium rare. Transfer to a heated platter and rest 10 minutes.
5. Carve meat from the bone and serve slices with sprinkle of salt and generous drizzle of olive oil.

Vitello Tonnato (Veal in Tuna Sauce)

Recipes for Vitello Tonnato regularly appear in Italian cookbooks. To the uninitiated, the combination of veal, tuna, and anchovies may seem unusual. The Romans learned long ago that tender mild veal is the perfect platform for the silky pungent tuna and anchovy sauce. Splurge on the very best quality veal so that the final result is nearly fork-tender. This pretty summer dish is served cold or at room temperature and can be prepared up to a day in advance of serving.

Ingredients

2 pounds boned and tied veal eye round

One 7-ounce can tuna in oil

1 onion, peeled and quartered

1 carrot, quartered

1 bay leaf

2 whole cloves

10 whole peppercorns

1 teaspoon salt

1 ½ cups dry white wine

1 ½ cups chicken broth

2 egg yolks

1 cup olive oil

One 12-ounce can tuna in oil

2 anchovies

3 tablespoon lemon juice

2 tablespoons capers

1 hardboiled egg, sieved (mashed through a strainer)

Preparation

Serves 6-8

1. Place veal, 7 ounces of tuna, onion, carrot, bay leaf, cloves, peppercorns, salt, wine, and chicken broth in a large saucepan.
2. Bring to boil, reduce heat to low. Cover and simmer 45 minutes.
3. Transfer meat to a large shallow bowl. Strain broth over meat. Cover and refrigerate until well chilled.
4. Place egg yolks in blender and process until pale and very thick.
5. Add olive oil in a thin stream to form a mayonnaise.
6. Add 12 ounces tuna, anchovies, and lemon. Blend to combine. Thin with small amount of chilled broth is necessary.
7. Remove veal from broth. Slice very thin.
8. Arrange slices neatly on a serving platter and cover with sauce. Reserve any extra sauce in a separate serving bowl.
9. Refrigerate, covered with plastic wrap, until ready to serve.
10. Garnish with capers and sieved egg.

Garlic
In ancient times, garlic was thought to be an aphrodisiac as it increased blood flow. It was mentioned on clay tablets and was used as collateral in financial agreements. Plant individual garlic cloves in September to form into bulbs with multiple cloves over the winter. Harvest the bulbs in June for year round use in the kitchen and more replanting in the fall.

Sautéed Broccoli Rabe with Caper Berries

All varieties of broccoli are found at the Roman table. Broccoli rabe has a distinctive slightly bitter taste, revealing its relation to the mustard family. The brininess of the caper berries and the sweetness of the orange provide a lively balance to this flavor-packed dish.

Ingredients

2 pounds broccoli rabe, ends trimmed and sliced into 2 inch sections

⅓ cup olive oil

2 cloves garlic, sliced thin

½ cup caper berries

⅔ cup dry white wine

¼ teaspoon red pepper flakes

Salt to taste

1 orange, zested and juiced

Preparation
Serves 4-6

1. Heat oil in large skillet until shimmering.
2. Add garlic and broccoli rabe. Sauté 3 minutes over medium heat, stirring constantly.
3. Lower heat. Add caper berries, wine, red pepper, salt, and orange zest. Simmer until broccoli rabe is crisp tender, 3-5 minutes. Wine should be mostly evaporated.
4. Transfer to a serving bowl and drizzle with orange juice.

Farro and Green Bean Salad

Farro has been cultivated for thousands of years and has lately seen a resurgence in popularity. Also known as spelt, it is related to wheat but is more nutritious and less refined. This hearty flavorful salad is nearly a meal unto itself, and a great vegetarian entrée.

Ingredients

1 cup farro

½ pound fresh haricot verts (very thin green beans)

⅓ cup extra virgin olive oil

3 large shallots, thinly sliced

3 cremini mushrooms, thinly sliced

1 clove garlic, minced

3 tablespoons balsamic vinegar

1 tablespoon fresh thyme leaves

1½ teaspoon salt and ½ teaspoon pepper, in total

½ cup fresh mint, roughly chopped

Preparation
Serves 4-6

1. In a medium saucepan, bring a quart of water to a rolling boil. Add farro and 1 teaspoon salt. Reduce to a simmer and cook, uncovered until *al dente*, 20 to 30 minutes depending on the grain. Drain and reserve.
2. Trim ends from green beans and slice into 1 inch pieces.
3. In a separate saucepan bring 2-3 cups water and remaining salt to a vigorous boil. Add green beans and cook 5 minutes. Drain, rinse under cold water, and reserve.
4. Heat 1-2 tablespoons olive oil in a sauté pan. Add shallots and mushrooms and cook over a medium high heat, stirring constantly, until lightly browned and juices have evaporated. Transfer to a small bowl.
5. In a medium bowl, whisk together remaining oil, vinegar, garlic, and thyme. Add farro, green beans, shallots, and mushrooms. Toss gently and serve garnished with mint.

Pignoli Cookies

The aroma of these traditional cookies is intoxicating. The deft combination of almond, pine nuts, and sugars is heavenly. No wonder they have been served for centuries.

Ingredients

Two 8-ounce cans almond paste

½ cup granulated sugar

1 cup confectioner's sugar

4 egg whites, beaten well

1 ½ cups pine nuts

Preparation

1. Preheat oven to 325 degrees.
2. Line 2 cookie sheets with parchment.
3. Mix almond paste and granulated sugar in stand mixer or food processor until smooth.
4. Add confectioner's sugar and ½ egg whites. Mix until smooth.
5. Whisk remaining egg whites in shallow bowl until frothy.
6. Place pine nuts in a separate shallow bowl.
7. With lightly floured hands, form dough into 1 inch balls.
8. Dip balls in egg white, roll in pine nuts, and place on lined cookie sheet.
9. Bake 15-18 minutes until lightly browned. Cool on cookie sheet 1 minute, then transfer to wire rack. Cool completely before storing in airtight container.

Yield 3 dozen

Pine Nuts
Pine Nuts (or *pignoli*) are the edible seeds of certain pine trees—in North America, the pinyon pine. Cones must be exposed to heat and each nut cracked open without damaging the kernel, which explains why the nuts are so expensive. Different varieties are found in Asia and Europe. Pine nuts, unlike other nuts, absorb the taste of other ingredients and so have been described as culinary chameleons.

Recipe Index

Metric Conversions

International cuisine requires international units of measurement. If you prefer metric units for measuring, the following conversions will be helpful.

TEMPERATURE
To convert from Fahrenheit to Celsius:
1) take the temperature in Fahrenheit and subtract 32
2) divide by 1.8 and the result is degrees Celsius

WEIGHT
Weights can be converted with the following table.

Note that the ounces referred to in this table are not the same as fluid ounces.

Weight Conversions

Customary Quantity	Metric Equivalent
1 ounce	28 g
4 ounces or ¼ pound	113 g
⅓ pound	150 g
8 ounces or ½ pound	230 g
⅔ pound	300 g
12 ounces or ¾ pound	340 g
1 pound or 16 ounces	450 g
2 pounds	900 g

LIQUIDS, HERBS, AND SPICES
Liquids can be converted to Liters or milliliters with the following table. Small volumes (less than about 1 fluid ounce or 2 tablespoons) of ingredients such as salt, herbs, spices, baking powder, etc. should also be converted with this table.

Volume Conversions

Customary Quantity	Metric Equivalent
1 teaspoon	5 ml
1 tablespoon or ½ fluid ounce	15 ml
1 fluid ounce or ⅛ cup	30 ml
¼ cup or 2 fluid ounces	60 ml
⅓ cup	80 ml
½ cup or 4 fluid ounces	120 ml
⅔ cup	160 ml
¾ cup or 6 fluid ounces	180 ml
1 cup or 8 fluid ounces or half a pint	240 ml
1½ cups or 12 fluid ounces	350 ml
2 cups or 1 pint or 16 fluid ounces	475 ml
3 cups or 1½ pints	700 ml
4 cups or 2 pints or 1 quart	950 ml
4 quarts or 1 gallon	3.8 ml

Note
In cases where higher precision is not justified, it may be convenient to round these conversions off as follows:
    1 cup = 250 ml
    1 pint = 500 ml
    1 quart = 1 L
    1 gallon = 4 L

Weight of Common Ingredients in Grams

OTHER NON-LIQUID INGREDIENTS

Non-liquid ingredients specified in our recipes by volume (if more than about 2 tablespoons or 1 fluid ounce) may be converted to weight with the following table. If you need to convert an ingredient that is not in this table, the safest thing to do is to measure it with a traditional measuring cup and then weigh the results with a metric scale. In a pinch, you can use the weight conversion table on the previous page.

Weights of Common Ingredients in Grams

Ingredient	1 cup	3/4 cup	2/3 cup	1/2 cup	1/3 cup	1/4 cup	2 Tbsp
Flour, all purpose (wheat)	120 g	90 g	80 g	60 g	40 g	30 g	15 g
Flour, well sifted all purpose (wheat)	110 g	80 g	70 g	55 g	35 g	27 g	13 g
Sugar, granulated cane	200 g	150 g	130 g	100 g	65 g	50 g	25 g
Confectioner's sugar (cane)	100 g	75 g	70 g	50 g	35 g	25 g	13 g
Brown sugar, packed firmly	180 g	135 g	120 g	90 g	60 g	45 g	23 g
Corn meal	160 g	120 g	100 g	80 g	50 g	40 g	20 g
Corn starch	120 g	90 g	80 g	60 g	40 g	30 g	15 g
Rice, uncooked	190 g	140 g	125 g	95 g	65 g	48 g	24 g
Macaroni, uncooked	140 g	100 g	90 g	70 g	45 g	35 g	17 g
Couscous, uncooked	180 g	135 g	120 g	90 g	60 g	45 g	22 g
Oats, uncooked quick	90 g	65 g	60 g	45 g	30 g	22 g	11 g
Table salt	300 g	230 g	200 g	150 g	100 g	75 g	40 g
Butter	240 g	180 g	160 g	120 g	80 g	60 g	30 g
Vegetable shortening	190 g	140 g	125 g	95 g	65 g	48 g	24 g
Chopped fruits and vegetables	150 g	110 g	100 g	75 g	50 g	40 g	20 g
Nuts, chopped	150 g	110 g	100 g	75 g	50 g	40 g	20 g
Nuts, ground	120 g	90 g	80 g	60 g	40 g	30 g	15 g
Bread crumbs, fresh, loosely packed	60 g	45 g	40 g	30 g	20 g	15 g	8 g
Bread crumbs, dry	150 g	110 g	100 g	75 g	50 g	40 g	20 g
Parmesan cheese, grated	90 g	65 g	60 g	45 g	30 g	22 g	11g